We Are Shiloh:

Stories of the Shiloh Children's Home

Andrew M. Lepper

Acknowledgments

Thank you to Megan Preedy. She is the glue that keeps NLO together in the US. Her official title is Donor Engagement Coordinator but it should be "Wonder Woman." She does it all. My sincerest heartfelt appreciation for all you do.

Thank you also to Michelle Parnell. She has been crucial in getting this new book in your hands. She has poured through every book to find the right stories to include here. She has committed countless hours to editing and tweaking. This book would not have come together had she not been diligent in helping create it.

An immense thank you to Scott Cuzzo. He is my designer extraordinaire. His cover art sets the precedents for what lies in the stories. The old adage goes that you cant judge a book by its cover. But with Scott, the cover is intertwined with the integrity of the stories inside. Thank you Scott.

And finally, thank you to Susan. She is the rock that keeps Shiloh together. She leads our home with humility and grace. She is the standard of hard work that our boys model themselves after. She is able to embrace any difficulties that come our way and helps to keep all of us sane during trying times. None of this would be possible without Susan. She is our Mama Bear. Everyone is better for knowing Susan. She loves fiercely and will hold you accountable. She has high standards for these boys but also has the grace and wisdom to hold their hand when they fall short. If Susan is on your side then you have a fiercely loyal friend until the day you die. We love you Susan. We are glad you are on our side.

Contents

Acknowledgements i

Introduction 1

Section 1: History of Shiloh

1. Meet Andy, Susan, and Micah Lepper 5

2. What's in a Name 11

3. Birth of Lovoso.. 15

Section 2: Daily Life

4. Day to Day 27

5. Prayer Room 31

6. Crops We Grow 35

7. Sustainability and a Goat..................................... 37

8. It Takes a Village 41

9. Animal Appreciation 45

10. At the playground.. 49

11. Baptismal Pool 53

12. We Grow Grass... 57

13. S'mores 61

14. Shiloh the Protector... 63

Section 3: The Boys

15. Addition and Subtractions 69

16. Meet Wally..73

17. We Are NOT Orphans..77

18. The Pain of Losing..29

19. Manu 85

20. Dinosaur Uncle 91

21. Welcome to the Family 93

22. Five New Boys...97

Section 4: Celebrations

23. Untold Story of the Best Birthday Party Ever 105

24. Simply Having a Wonderful Christmastime...................109

25. Birthdays Are Special...113

26. Birthday Bread...117

27. My 38th Birthday..121

28. Christmas Bikes for the Boys 123

29. WWE..127

30. My 41st Birthday Party 137

Section 5: Special Friends

31.Murghi Uncle & David's Guest Post 143

32. Kanti 147

33. Jesus Toffee 151

34. Grandma Judy 153

35. Thoughts from "Ken Uncle" 157

36. Jaimie's Story 163

Section 6: God's Provisions

37. Good Things Come 169

38. God Ain't Forgot Us Yet 171

39. Sometimes It's the Little Things 173

40. God Shows Up 177

41. Never Going Hungry 179

42. New Well 185

Section 7: From Our Hearts

43. Confession Time 189

44. One of the Greatest Days of My Life 191

45. The Weight of Struggles 201

46. Closing 205

Introduction

Thank you for taking the time to read this book. Let me give you a little heads up before you start. This book is a compilation of stories from my first four books about Shiloh. Instead of having to read through 4 books, we have compiled our favorite stories in one place. The stories are in order of subject matter, not in order of when the story happened. The first book we released was a collection of blog posts from our website. This is why a story may reference blogs or Facebook. Also bear in mind; we have had our children's home for eight years at the time of the release of this book. During that time, a lot has changed. We have seen children come and go. In the beginning, we started with 18 boys. At our height, we had 48 boys. We have had all different amounts in between. Keep that in mind if you read a chapter that mentions 18 boys, but the next chapter mentions 30 boys. We intended to structure this book in a way as to give you a broad understanding of what God has done in our home for the last eight years. There are times in the book where we have no animals. But there are also times in the book where we have over 800 animals. Just keep in mind that each chapter is a small snapshot of our home. It is 100% true, but details may not seem to flow with dates and numbers. Thank you for your understanding.

It is incredible to look back and see where God has brought us. It is amazing to see the ways that God provided. It has been amazing to revisit these stories and see God's faithfulness. It is also empowering to think about where he will take us next. We have a long way to go and a lot to do. Please enjoy these stories and hop on the bus. It is going to be a wild ride

Section 1 :
History of Shiloh

Chapter 1

Our Story: Andy, Susan, and Micah Lepper

During my freshman year of college (1995), a guy named Clayton King came to Campbell University, where I studied and spoke to one of the Bible studies I was in. He let us know that he was starting a summer camp, and anyone who wanted to be summer camp staff could be involved. So, I signed up to be a staff member for Crossroads Summer Camp.

I was on that first staff of Crossroads summer camp in NC. I fell in love with Clayton – he's an awesome guy. During that summer camp, he told me, "Andy, you're going to go to India with me." I responded that I had no desire to go to India, and he encouraged me to pray about it. He told me to plan on going to India, and if God shut any door, then don't go, but not to tell God what to do before I'd even asked Him.

That got me to India the first time in November 1997. The first time I was in India, I knew that my life was changed forever.

I knew that's what I wanted to do with the rest of my life. I didn't know how it was going to happen – I just knew.

I kept going back to India every few months for Christmas, summer breaks, etc., carrying other college students with me. So far, I've hosted or led 300-400 people here in India. I just really fell in love with India. I knew that one day, I would live in India and run an orphanage or something because the first time I went to India, I served at the largest orphanage in the world where at one point, they had 2800 children.

I met Susan in 1999 – we didn't date or fall in love immediately. I was in charge of leading these teams, and she was a Bible college graduate and was in charge of the guest house there at the orphanage. So we interacted with one another regularly. I kept falling more and more in love with India, and I didn't know what I wanted. I didn't know if God would bring me a wife from a college or seminary or where, but I kept getting to know Susan more.

One day I realized she's who I wanted to spend the rest of my life with. So in April 2002, I asked her to marry me, and we got married on March 9, 2003. We lived in India until August 2004, not by choice. We thought we could go to the US embassy, tell them that she's my wife, get her passport stamped, and head to America, but it didn't work that way.

It was less than two years after 9-11, and so many new laws had been enacted with border security. They were doing more intensive background checks and vetting everyone. It took us a year and a half after we got married to get back to the US.

We moved to the US in August 2004 with the sole intention that we would get her US citizenship, which isn't automatic just because she married a US citizen. So we worked hard and took a lot of trips back to India. The whole time we were supporting orphans in India and Haiti – but we were focused on India.

Dr. Samuel Thomas came one day and gave us the option to help with a children's home. He said there was a children's home that needed leadership in North India. There were actually two homes that needed help so we could choose whether we wanted to go to Alwar, Rajasthan or Delhi. I prayed about it – but at first, I didn't want to go to either one because I wanted to go back to South India where Susan was from because when Susan was eight years old, her father left her family – and her mother was left alone to care for three young girls.

When we got married, my mother in law was making $8 a month! When Susan was eight years old, her mother couldn't afford to take care of any of them. So her older sister went to be a servant in someone's home, and her younger sister was only two years old at the time, so she just bounced around the village to other family members who could help take care of her. My mother in law went to work in someone's home also. That left Susan. A pastor agreed to take Susan and took her as far away from her home as you can get and still be in India. She left South India and went to North India – a three-day train ride – and literally didn't see her mother again until the day we got married.

So Susan was raised at a children's home, and I wanted to go to South India to reconcile Susan with her family. There are orphanages all over India, but I thought it would be where God would lead me.

We had a choice between two places in North India. I had a dream one night, and I just felt the nudging to go to Alwar – my dream asked me what I was waiting on....that tomorrow isn't promised...there are boys that need a father and mother now...what are you waiting on? So I remember waking up and telling Susan that we should go to Alwar and take over a children's home that was already there.

In August 2012, we took over this children's home, and we named it Shiloh. Shiloh was a city in the Old Testament of the Bible that was known as a place of rest for weary travelers. This is what I envisioned for our children's home, so we named our campus Shiloh. But we had things to take care of in the US first. We owned our home in NC, and we decided that since we had no income coming in and No Longer Orphans was in its infancy, that we would keep our house and rent it out – that can be our retirement plan.

Susan had just signed a contract to be a nanny, so we knew that would help us as we got this children's home started. So Susan was in the US working, and I would come to India and live here for 3 months, then go home and live in the US for 3 months...back and forth. We did this for the first year of Shiloh.

As we packed up our house to get it ready to rent, I ran across my journal from the first time that I came to India in 1997. This was now 15 years after my first trip to India. All I knew at that point was that I felt led to Alwar, but everything was a little unknown....not sure why I picked Alwar over Delhi. Why didn't I stick to my guns and go to South India?

I ran across my journal from 1997, and one of the days that I was here in Rajasthan, I had written in the journal that we'd traveled a lot and been to about 10 other places. I had been to Jalawar, Alwar, Tonk, Deoli, Bundi, Newai, Rapirua, Piploda, Jaipur and Kota. But I wrote in my journal that out of all of those places, I'd felt God's presence the most in Alwar. So I asked God in my journal from 1997 to please send me back to Alwar. That's before I'd even met Susan – and no one had ever seen this journal. I'd forgotten about it. But God didnt forget. He sent had been preparing us. He sent me a dream in the right time. And He fulfilled my prayer request from 15 years earlier. Even though I had forgotten, God was faithful. This journal was a reminder to me about God fulfilling His promises to us.

So I started traveling over to India and slowly becoming a father for the boys. It took Susan another year because of her job, but she joined me right before Christmas 2014. We've been here ever since.

We've got a 20-acre piece of farmland here, and a 30,000 square foot building – all of this was entrusted to us to care for the home we have here. We don't own the land or the building, but God has allowed us to be here in this time, for this purpose – to be able to care for the boys. It's not over yet – we plan on being here as long as God will have us, and we love every minute that we're here.

A caveat to the story is that we got married in 2003, and we immediately started trying to have children. But we couldn't have children. While we were in the US, we still couldn't get pregnant – we went to doctors all over NC, India, everywhere and could not have a baby. We even went to a doctor at Duke who told us that it was improbable we'd ever get pregnant. I remember Susan telling the doctor that not only would she have a baby, but that baby would have blond hair and blue eyes. Susan got here in December of 2014, we had a son, Micah, in September 2015. It was a big answer to prayer. He was born with blonde hair and blue eyes.

Both of our lives had led to us moving to India and having our own home with all of these children – maybe it was a stress release because we had a family. Once we moved here and were in the middle of God's will, we got pregnant almost immediately. Twelve years after we got married, we had our son.

Thank you for supporting us as we continue to serve at Shiloh Children's Home.

Chapter 2

What's in a Name?

I love naming things. I named my first truck Molly after my kindergarten crush. I love giving nicknames to friends like my college friend, Benjamin, or as I called him, Ben Jammin. I love naming regular old stuff...mostly, I name stuff Elvis. He was my first music love, ya know? I called my dog Elvis, my guitar Elvis, and my first laptop was Elvis, ad nauseum. I have had fun naming festivals that I started...Does anyone remember the Peacemaker Festivals? I had a record company called PeaceFreek.

I ran an organization called Tyro Mavin Worldwide. Currently, we have a jewelry company called Chunky Junk, a social business called LOVOSO, and our non-profit to orphans, of course, is No Longer Orphans. I love the process of naming things: the research phase, picking out possibilities, and the people's reaction when you give them possible options. Even the naming of this book was somewhat of a competition from longtime supporters of No Longer Orphans. It is no secret at the orphanage that we are expanding and will have various initiatives that enable us to become sustainable. I want to introduce you to each of those initiatives, their names, and how I set about naming them.

First off, as you may know, the actual name of the children's home is Shiloh. One of my top three artists of the last twenty years is Andrew Peterson. On his first album, he has a song entitled "Shiloh." This was the name of his childhood home.

The song calls to you as you listen, "Get on home to Shiloh." I thought it a fitting tribute to thank Andrew by naming the orphanage Shiloh. As I did a little research, the name became a better fit than I had first thought. In the Old Testament, there was a city named Shiloh. As one historian noted, Shiloh was known as a "place of rest for weary travelers." Wow, what better moniker could we possibly find? We genuinely want to be a place where weary travelers and friends alike can come and rest their weary bones while helping us transform the lives of these amazing boys. Thanks so much, Andrew Peterson, for being a part of my life these last few years through your music. Our boys adore every album you have done. I would highly recommend that everyone "discover" Andrew Peterson, if you have not done so already, and buy all of his albums.

The second initiative we are building is the auto initiative. Although it is affectionately known as the Auto Initiative here, once we have our fleet of cars, we will need to call it something in India. We have settled on Sound Travels. This is a play on word in three ways.

First of all, sound indeed does travel. Second, "sound" also means stable, competent, and reliable. The third way is because of what the initiative is named after. Another one of my influential artists that have impacted my life is Jon Foreman of Switchfoot. He brilliantly wrote a song called "The Sound."

My favorite line from the song is, "There is no song louder than love." What we are trying to do with the auto initiative is to share the love and care for our boys in creative ways. The "sound" of our love should be more than just spoken words. It should be in our every action and thought. Thus, the naming of the Auto Initiative is Sound Travels. The Auto Initiative is meant to be a way for us to impact our local community and sustainably provide for ourselves by having a fleet of auto-rickshaws and small cars that we rent out to people who otherwise have no transportation.

Finally, we come to our animals and the farm. We have a fast-growing herd of animals that currently number two water buffalo, three rabbits, eight dogs, and twenty-five chickens. The goats and other barnyard favorites will quickly follow. We may even have a camel in the coming year. We also have twenty acres of farmland where we grow a bunch of crops like wheat, guar, mustard, dal, and corn. I thought about the naming of this farm more than the others because it's the closest to my heart.

I have settled on naming it "Resplendent Farms." The word resplendent means "to shine brilliantly, be radiant, dazzling, gleaming." This epitomizes the life I want for my boys. I want them to be the shining glory of our Risen Lord. Resplendent is a tribute to my favorite author, artist, singer, songwriter, poet of all time, Bill Mallonee. Bill was the stalwart behind the

Vigilantes of Love. They recorded one of my favorite songs of all time, "Resplendent." The song is about triumph through heartache, joy from pain. It reminds me of the dustbowl generation who literally had nothing, but somehow many of them, through gritted teeth, chose joy. My own grandfather lost his first wife and firstborn to disease. This is similar to the story of my boys. Even though the world has discarded them and expects them to fail, they are resplendent. I implore you to listen to the song and rejoice with me that we are all resplendent despite our shortcomings. Thank you so much, Mr. Bill, for your lyrics that have been a central guiding rod in my life.

Please check out his stuff at http://billmalloneemusic. bandcamp.com/merch. Blessings to you if you fall in love with his music as much as I have. He has produced over 75 albums over the last twenty years. He doesn't know this, but I named my new motorcycle Mallonee.

So, there you have it - the new names and the reasons behind them. I introduce to you: Shiloh Children's Home, Sound Travels, Resplendent Farms.

Chapter 3

Birth of Lovoso

We have had a church from the Augusta, Georgia area visit us for the last few years. The church is Kiokee Baptist Church. One of the Kiokee team members was Brian DeJong. Brian's father grew up as a missionary kid in South Africa. Brian moved to Africa when he was two. They moved back to Harlem, Georgia, when he was eight years old. They once again moved back to Africa, this time Kenya, when Brian was 13. He went to a boarding school where he learned woodworking.

He now owns his own custom woodworking business, which was his childhood dream. I had not met him before he visited us one April, but I had some correspondence before the team arrived. Since Brian is a master woodworker, he wanted to work closely with a few boys to teach them a crash course in old-school woodworking. He wanted to teach old techniques like dovetailing, mortise and tenon, and how to use hand tools to create and not rely on modern power equipment.

We knew that the time would be limited, so we decided to

offer it to just two boys. Of course, when I asked all of the boys if they were interested, they all said yes. So, I gave the boys more details about what Brian would be teaching and told them that they had to provide me with a written application on why they felt they were the best candidate. We got a few applications, but only three were genuinely interested. So, we settled on 3.

I desired that these three boys would use the week with Brian to be the catalyst to do woodworking for their careers, possibly. All three boys mentioned that in their letter. They all wanted to learn so they could make furniture for a living. Now that we had chosen the three boys who would be part of the project, we decided to create a list of supplies that Brian would need to hit the ground running. He sent me a sheet with various wood needs.

We don't have a Home Depot or Lowes, so I went to the only wood store I knew. I passed along my sheet with my wood needs, and the owner quoted me over $800. This was for just enough wood to make two cornhole boards. There was no way that I was spending $800 in India to make two cornhole boards. No way! So, I did the only other thing I knew to do. I went to the local scrapyard that I had been to countless times for my projects.

This "scrapyard" was just an open field by the highway in our village. It was about the size of a football field and was filled with broken pallets and discarded wood of all sizes. It is very common in India to cook over a fire, so this field was where many people would buy their wood. It was sold by the kilogram. Because of this, the area was usually filled with people taking screws and nails out of boards so they wouldn't have to pay for the extra weight that the nail or screw represented.

I went out there the week before Brian and the team arrived. I carried the three boys who would be learning as well as a couple of our male staff. We knew exactly what we needed, but it took us almost 4 hours to dig through the mountain of boards to find the right dimension wood. It then took us another hour to remove all the nails, screws, nuts, and bolts. The boards probably weighed 5 pounds less, once we had all the metal removed. We had everything weighed and all the wood we needed weighed well over 50 pounds. I was a little worried about the possible price, especially after getting a quote for $800 for the same amount of wood. But I was pleasantly surprised when it was only $20. Of course, we had to work very hard for that $20 worth of wood, but it was still better than paying $800. And we had an experience we will never forget.

When Brian arrived with the team, he set out teaching the boys the art of old-school woodworking. He showed them how to make dovetails in wood as well as mortise and tenons. He meticulously worked with each boy to make sure that they knew each technique. He only had five days, but he made sure they understood the fine details of a few things rather than teaching them many things they would never remember.

It was a very successful week, and those three boys learned a lot. They began to make little benches, tables, and chairs. They were excellent quality even from the beginning, Brian was a great teacher. As they went on, their skill improved. They enjoyed it so much that they started to think of woodworking as a potential career. So, I racked my brain for ways to help. I knew that I could not bring it with me to the United States. It was too bulky, and the cost of baggage fees or shipping would eat so much into the profit that the boys really wouldn't benefit.

I spent a few days carrying their handiworks around our local city. I was dumbfounded at the response. I expected people to be a little more open to beautiful handcrafted tables and benches like they were making. Bear in mind that this is, of course, sought after in the United States. People appreciate the time and skill it takes to make a bench. And they appreciate the dovetails.

For those that may not know, dovetailing is the old school art of connecting the joints of a piece of wood primarily through engineered pressure and force rather than with nails or screws. It takes skill to do this. I thought the local Indian businesses would appreciate that. But boy was I wrong. Many of them offered me half of what I asked, but not because they were trying to negotiate. Most said that they wouldn't pay much at all because it didn't have nails or screws. So, the skill and craftsmanship were lost on them. They just didn't get it.

After my rejection of trying to sell the furniture locally, I gave up. I wasn't able to sell it locally, and I knew I couldn't and shouldn't ship it to the US. My family took a trip to the United States soon after. The boys' woodworking was the last thing on my mind. About halfway through our journey in early May, we stayed at some of our friend's house. They are both doctors. The husband, Mark, deals with a lot of trauma cases at his hospital. I asked him how he manages to deal with the pressure of all that while still being a great husband and loving father. He told me that one of the ways that he deals with the stress is to turn pens. The moment he said the words "turn pens," I felt like my head would explode. I knew exactly what he meant, but to make sure I wasn't misunderstanding, I asked him to repeat.

He told me that he had a lathe and that when he had the time and was stressed that he would make wooden pens. When he said this, I felt like the world's biggest light bulb had just been lit above my head. "THAT'S IT!" I shouted. Susan thought I was crazy. I knew at that exact moment that I needed to learn how to make pens so that I could train the three boys. This was something that they could learn fast, which applied to what they already had a passion for.

But most importantly, it would be super easy to carry it in my luggage when I traveled back and forth to the United States.

The hardest part would be finding someone to teach me. Or so I thought. I immediately called Brian and asked him if he knew of anyone that could show me how to make pens before we returned to India so that I could pass the skill on to the boys. He responded that He knew how to make pens and that he could teach me. My laughing response was, "If you know how to make pens, then why didn't you teach THAT to the boys?"

We both had a good laugh. Within two days, I was in Brian's workshop, learning all that he knew. It had been a few years since he had done it, but you could tell that he had the skill.

He quickly remembered everything and taught me all he knew. I was mesmerized as the first pen I saw him make took him only 10 minutes from start to finish. He told me of the different things you could build on the lathe that the boys could learn. He quickly made me a keychain and a spinning top. But I decided then that I wanted to perfect the art of pen-making before moving on to other things.

Brian was the perfect teacher, but I wanted to learn from others as well. I started spending 12-14 hours a day watching Youtube videos from different pen makers. Each one had different techniques. My favorite pen maker is a guy named Bob, who has a Youtube channel called RJBWoodturner. I learned a lot of hands-on stuff from his channel once I returned to India. Of course, Brian wasn't close for me to watch him work, and often because of the time difference, I could not pick his brain. So, I watched Bob's videos that covered every stage of pen making. After a couple of months, I started to have my own style. I just did what worked best for me since I didn't have access in India to many of the supplies and tools that are more readily available in the United States. I ended up coming up with a process that was up to 50 steps depending on what kind of finish I put on my pens. It was quite a journey to get to that point. I did get to the point where I could make a pen as fast as Brian.

Once I was confident in my pen making abilities, it was time to teach the boys. Just before that, I showed my best friend, JP. I wanted to have someone who could train the boys alongside me. And I needed to have someone that could work with the boys during one of my many trips to the US. So, I took a couple of weeks and taught JP everything I knew up to that point. We

We Are Shiloh: Stories of the Shiloh Children's Home

both worked hard to transfer one of our storage rooms into a proper workshop. I was unable to find a lathe in India, and I was scared to bring a powered one from the US because of the electricity difference. With Brian's help, I found a lathe called a "hobby lathe." It wasn't powered. It was mainly a bracket that you could fit a power drill to convert the drill into a lathe. This wasn't ideal, but I knew that it would suffice until we could find an alternative. I had brought two from the US, so JP and I taught the boys how to turn a pen by making one a lathe as they sat at an adjacent table and mimicked what we did on the other machine. Before long, the boys were off and running. They loved making pens. But making pens isn't just the thrill of using the lathe. Part of my 50-step process includes finding the right wood, cutting it to size, and many steps preparing it to be turned. Even after turning it to the proper size, there are steps to sand, finish, and polish the pen in order for it to last. The boys began to be active in every part of the 50 steps. I have refined the steps down to 30, but in the beginning, it was more time-consuming.

One day as I was working in the workshop, I began to think about all the other boys at the Shiloh Children's Home. I have told them countless times that I have enough love for all of them, but I don't have enough time. I always feel like I want to spend more time with them, but it can be hard when I travel so much.

I began to think about the lack of time I get to spend with the boys. I started to think of all the time I got to spend with my father. He taught me many life lessons like time management, discipline, integrity, working with others, etc. The life lessons he taught me are innumerable. But when I dwelled on it, they all came from a commonplace. I learned every one of them mainly from working WITH my dad. He was always the hardest working person I knew. He would rise before the sun daily and wouldn't return from work at his furniture store until long after the sun was down. I realized in middle school that if I wanted to spend time with my dad that I had to go where he was. So, I did.

I started working with him and for him from the time I was 13 years old. When I got to work after school, I remember for one of my birthdays he brought me to the warehouse where his other workers had just unloaded a full semi-trailer of furniture. He handed me a new box cutter that was covered in wrapping paper. When he handed it to me, he winked and said, "Happy Birthday, son. I give you the gift of hard work."

I am sure that my mother made sure that I had lots of other presents that year. But I will never forget that box cutter or the greatest gift anyone has ever given me, the gift of hard work. My father mimicked the great quote, "The reward for hard work well done is the opportunity to do more." When I remember back on that, I began to think of all of my boys. If I have so much love but so little time, how can I pass along all of the things that my father passed on to me? I realized that the workshop that I was standing in was the answer.

I decided that I should open the workshop to any boy who was willing to come and learn. The only requirement was that they needed to at least be in high school. The first time I invited them in EVERY qualified boy came. We had 14 boys total at that first workshop meeting. I laid out the expectations and possibilities. I told the boys that they had to earn the right to make a pen. It was a privilege to make a pen, not a right. Making a pen quickly became a rite of passage.

The boys knew that they had to master all of the lower steps in the process before they could turn a pen. They started out sweeping the floors, then helping select the wood. They moved on to measuring and then hand cutting the wood. Within six months, every one of the 14 boys could make a pen from start to finish. And they were good at it. Every boy can make a pen just as good if not better than me, JP, or Brian DeJong. I am so proud of them. But what I am most proud of is our little workshop that has turned my 14 boys into 14 young men who carry themselves with grace, integrity, and determination. 14 boys who know the value of hard work and the value of a team. This is what I am most proud of.

We decided that the best way to move forward was by treating this as a legitimate company. We didn't want to incorporate as a nonprofit because nonprofits have limitations when it comes to selling goods. We wanted to be a social business. My definition of a social business is "A company that uses its net profits for social needs." For us, social needs are caring for our orphans and helping widows and at-risk all around us. We decided to donate all of the net profits of our company to meet these needs. I had been holding on to the name LOVOSO for almost ten years. The letters in LOVOSO mean Love Orphans, Visit Orphans, Serve Orphans.

LOVOSO was to be the name of our handicraft business. Before you think that this is just a clever way to get free labor from the boys for making the pens that we sell, let me tell you what it means to them. We discussed with the boys that they would earn $1 for every pen that they turned. To put this into perspective, laborers in our village make $3 per day. Even with school, a boy could make five pens per day. I not only wanted the boys to benefit from turning a pen, but I wanted each of them to benefit from all of the other steps. We decided that we would dedicate another $1 from every pen to be split amongst the boys. How this worked was that we had the boys keep track of their time every day. We also kept track of every pen that was finished. Then each boy would get paid based on his time working. For example, we calculated that all the boys worked 1000 hours one month. We also made 1000 pens that month with each pen giving $1 into the word "pot." So, $1000 was split between 1000 hours, meaning that each hour worked was worth $1. Bear in mind that people work in fields 12 hours a day for $3. Once we had the value of each hour, the boys were paid based on how many hours they worked. I am not crazy enough to pass out that money to my boys, though. For reasons I cannot explain here, it is not wise for us to give them money. I told the boys that 50% of the money they earned would go into a fund for their college or start their lives. The other 50% was available to them immediately, and they could purchase anything they wanted through our canteen. If they wanted new shoes, then they could use that money and go with me to buy them. They loved this. They had access to some cash at that moment, as well as saving up money for college. This made them want to work even harder. They were so proud of the fact that they had a skill that could benefit them for life.

As we stand, we have made over 12,000 pens. Our pens are some of the best quality but lowest priced you will ever find. We benefit from the low cost of local wood and our labor cost being low. We are frugal and work hard at not being wasteful with our supplies. We are confident in our price point. At this stage, we are in a dilemma because we are making a lot more pens than we are selling. I try to sell as many pens as I can when I am in the US, but my trips are more about sharing our work than trying to sell. We will find the right balance. As of the release of this new book, the boys have learned how to do other woodworking like making guitars, bowls, rings, etc. We want to expand Lovoso to include other at-risk people. We would love for it to branch out to at-risk women and men who need skills training. Please pray that Lovoso can continue to train and mentor these young men and grow to teach and help as many people in India as possible. We don't want to give a handout. We want to give a hand up. If you are interested in what we currently have available, please check our website at www.lovoso.com or send us an email at info@ lovoso.com.

We Are Shiloh: Stories of the Shiloh Children's Home

Section 2:
Daily Life

Chapter 4

Day to Day

Many people have asked me what a typical day looks like here at the orphanage. Occasionally my own wife asks, "What exactly DID you do today?" Even though every day varies, here is just a glimpse:

5:30 Staff wakes up and begin cooking breakfast for children

5:45 Boys wake up and pray

6:45 Boys prepare for school

7:15 Boys eat breakfast

7:45 Boys head out to school

8:30-9 Staff prayer

9-12 I personally spend time working the land and animals and other labor projects around the building, including the laundry. I do, on average, 30 loads of laundry a week. SERIOUSLY.

12-3 I travel into the city to buy supplies. With 20,000 square feet and 35 people living here, there are

 always things to buy.

3 pm Boys arrive from school and begin homework

4 pm Boys start their work and chores and have canteen

5 pm Boys play cricket and marbles and whatever else they want

6 pm We have one hour of prayer time

7 pm Boys eat dinner

8 pm Boys continue their homework

9 pm Boys go to bed, and my day begins.

When I say my day begins, I mean, according to American time. This is when I do all of my writing (which is right now.) I spend time assisting teams and people who will be coming to visit us. I get the honor of interacting with our donors who make this whole thing happen. I also have the opportunity to unwind and read.

Around midnight, I emerge from my office and lock everything up and head to bed. I am a person that thrives on eight hours of sleep. I can function with little sleep only by God's grace, even though I am always the first one up and the last one down.

I haven't had eight hours of sleep, or anything close to it, since coming to Shiloh. My Fitbit says I average about two hours and thirty minutes of sleep a night. Please be praying for us as we go through our day-to-day.

Chapter 5

Prayer Room

We have about twenty-eight rooms in our orphanage, give or take a closet or two. One of my first objectives was to re-work every room and plan what we should do for each. When I arrived here, most of the rooms stored junk. I got rid of most of it and consolidated the rest. With the remaining empty rooms, I made four guest rooms and set aside one for an office. I allotted one for a study hall for the boys and one for a computer lab. We have a storeroom to keep our newly laid chicken eggs as well as their feed. In the future, there will be a music room and a sports equipment room.

By far, my favorite room, and my top priority was the prayer room. After months of trying to obtain the necessary items, we finished it as of yesterday. The room is not very big, but it is enough for us to fit and be cozy. I have placed twelve dry erase boards on the wall so we can record all of our prayer requests, and yours too. For our 6 pm prayer time, we come into the room and sing for about ten minutes. Then, we go one by one through the prayer requests on the boards. We have boards for requests from the United States, for Indian requests, and one specifically for the boys' personal requests.

Almost every boy is praying for the salvation of his family members or the protection of his family from persecution. That is their prayer requests.

When I was that age, I probably prayed for a bike or a girl to like me. These boys are praying that their families will come to know the one true God. Heart-wrenching and humbling. We also have a couple of boards of praises for when God answers our prayers.

After we pray, we sing, and we are done. One thing to note – I have encouraged the boys whenever they walk by the prayer room to stop in and quickly go down the list. For the last two days, I have observed boy after boy wander in for five or ten minutes and pray on their own.

How's your prayer life? I know mine could use some dedication like that. I wholeheartedly believe that God hears children's prayers faster than adults who have too much junk in the way. I mean, look at this verse, "See that you do not look down on one of these little ones. For I tell you that their angels in heaven always see the face of my Father in heaven." - Matthew 18:10" It says right there that their angels are hanging out with God himself, 24/7!

So, if you have a prayer request, send it our way. I have twenty-eight prayer warriors ready to intercede on your behalf. It is incredible what God is doing at our humble orphanage. The boys are growing, learning, and continuously on the move. They rise early and pray. They go to school all day, six days a week. They play hard and have more chores than I had at their age (it is a large facility). They worship like it's their job.

And they love, love, love. They love their families and each other and me.

Please don't let how awesome our boys are deceive you into stopping your prayers for them. We need your prayers now more than ever. We are surrounded by people who are far from like-minded. We are in a constant daily struggle to provide. Yet God miraculously provides. Every. Single. Day. Please don't stop praying. We need it!

Our boys are diligent in their prayer life. Our prayer room is filled with prayer requests that the boys go through individually and with passion. They reach their hands out to the names on our prayer wall, begging God to heal many from cancer, disease, and other sicknesses. They ask God to provide traveling mercies for those on journeys, and they pray for God to provide comfort and peace for grieving families. The boys pray this for you.

So, I once again beg you to remember our boys in prayer. Pray for their daily needs. Pray for their education. Pray for their future. Pray that God will use them mightily. If you have a specific prayer request, please let me know. The boys will intercede with passion for you. I pray you will do the same for them.

We Are Shiloh: Stories of the Shiloh Children's Home

Chapter 6

Crops We Grow

We have the awesome privilege to enjoy living on twenty-ish acres of land. Five of these acres are used for our building, driveway, and soccer field, leaving us with fifteen acres of agricultural land. We have two weather dynamics in our area. We have the highest recorded temperature in India at one hundred twenty-five degrees, but because of the monsoon season, we get a lot of rain in a short period of time. We have a similar average rainfall to Raleigh, North Carolina, although we have a desert-like climate for ten months of the year. This difficulty allows us to have plenty of well water but dry crops for most of the year, therefore, we are limited in what we plant and grow on the land.

Currently, we grow corn, wheat, mustard, bajra, corn, and guar. Guar is a vital crop because it is used in the oil industry, making it a very beneficial and prosperous crop to grow. It is a volatile crop, so it is hard to grow at times. Most of the time, we grow corn, wheat, and mustard.

We can mill mustard into oil, and the wheat and corn into flour. This helps us sustain the orphans; however, we do not make enough in the marketplace because of the low cost of the crops. We hope to convert two to three acres into a large garden that the boys can cultivate. With more attention, we will be able to grow onions, tomatoes, beans, okra, and watermelons, to name a few. We also want to have animals such as water buffaloes, goats, and chickens roaming free on our land. We will primarily use the animals for their milk and eggs.

We give God the glory that we have this remarkable amount of land to work with. Please join us in prayer that one day the property will be able to sustain us better.

Chapter 7

Sustainability and a Goat Named Mrs. Eatin'

God moves in mysterious ways, His wonders to perform. If you have read our website's funding page, you will soon realize how we operate and raise funds. For the most part, we do not share every need we have. We do this partly because of over-saturation. We do not want to be an organization that continually inundates you with plea after plea. No one likes that. Also, we do not share some of our immediate needs because we first take them to God. If He leads us to keep things quiet, we do.

We want to share some needs with you at this time based on the individual need, the pressing of God, and the encouragement of a few close friends of No Longer Orphans. But first, a sad but cool story that just happened. Last week, I received a frantic call from JP that our water buffalos, Lady and Agape, were missing. We had no idea what happened to them. Our first thought was that they were stolen, but it seems that after some time and investigation, the gate was inadvertently left open, and a couple of boys forgot to tie up the animals. Open gate=missing buffalos. We haven't found them and will likely never see them again. Grace applied to the boys who made a mistake, and new rules about open gates.

However, we are still saddened about the loss of our beloved buffalos. A church Sunday school donated the funds to purchase them, and we needed the animals. They provided milk for us every day, and we used the extra milk to sell and get funding for other food.

When I got the call from JP, I was in Tennessee visiting a bunch of families who have a heart for India and want to establish schools and orphanages. I shared the story with them. Many of the families have adopted from India. The following day, one of the girls who was adopted from India had her first birthday party in the United States. She turned five and had a fantastic party. In place of gifts, the family requested donations for our orphanage, and by the grace of God, $600 was given, which is precisely what we need to purchase a new buffalo.

The incident made us realize a few things. First, we want to be as close to fully sustainable as we can be, which means having multiple animals that we can milk or get eggs from. The loss of the buffalo hit us hard. We lost good income, and the boys are without their daily milk. Now, we are adding a section on the donate page to help us purchase a water buffalo. We need at least five water buffalos to help us towards sustainability.

Another cool thing happened while we were in Tennessee. We stayed with Tim and Liz Eaton, who are both teachers. Liz shared all about our orphanage with her 6th-grade class. The children wanted to take up an offering. Liz legally cannot have anything to do with it or encourage it, but the kids on their own took up an offering and gave it to Tim without Liz's knowledge or consent. The kids took up $122, which we are going to use to purchase a goat. Goats are around $100 in our area. We have decided to call the goat Mrs. Eatin', named after Liz and the fact that goats eat everything. We will post pics of Mrs. Eatin' and the buffalo as soon as we purchase them.

All that to say, we have added animals back to our donate page. If you feel led to help us purchase an animal, we will let you name it and also send a certificate signed by all of the boys in appreciation for partnering with us. The links to the animals are below. Who doesn't want to name a goat after their ex-girlfriend, angry boss, or your best friend?

We Are Shiloh: Stories of the Shiloh Children's Home

Chapter 8

It Takes a Village

As some of you may know, we have been back and forth the last year caring for the orphans. We were mostly in India, but it has been a year of transitions as we move over for good. That time is here, and we make the move next week. This next week will be exceptionally hectic, so I wanted to share this with you now.

You have heard the saying that it takes a village to raise a child. This is true. For us, our village is worldwide. We cannot do it without the broader community assisting us with prayers and donations. This is especially true this week, and I want to share this with you specifically.

Last week, I put up a post about how you can donate animals to our orphanage and name them in honor of whatever you want. A few did just that, and I want to share their stories. First off, the Brocato family has decided to donate a goat. The mother, Nicole, says her kids thought she was crazy when she told them. They will believe it soon enough when the goat is purchased, and they can see it for themselves. They are working on a name, and I will let you know as soon as they come up with something.

Crystal Perdue has donated five chickens and two pillow and sheet sets for the boys. Thank you so much, Crystal. Fresh eggs are the bee's knees!

Amanda Raines from Welcome Baptist Church in Greenville, South Carolina donated money for a goat. We have decided to name the goat "Manna" because God has provided. Amanda was telling me that her mother wrote a book entitled "Gathering Manna" to tell of the miraculous ways God has provided for her family. What a great honor to name a goat in remembrance that God is faithful. You can learn more of the full story and the book on their website -

http://www.gatheringmanna.org/

Finally, Susan and I were selling jewelry at a festival the other day to raise funds for the orphans. We were sharing space, selling Chunky Junk jewelry, and working next to a lovely couple who operated the Red Cross booth about the children. What a great day it was just talking and enjoying new friends! When we got home, we discovered they had donated money for a goat in remembrance of our brief time together. The goat will be named Wallace since that is the city where the festival was held. Thank you so much, Gerri and Dean Hanson, for the gift of Wallace.

See how easy it is to have an impact on our children??? For the time being, I am going to remove the goat donation button because three is precisely what we need for now. I will probably add it back at the end of the summer. In the meantime, remember that we still need at least two more water buffaloes and dozens of more chickens. Chickens are only $10 for two hens. Please help if you can. I will update this once I get situated and buy the five chickens and three goats.

Chapter 9

Animal Appreciation

This month, February is Animal Appreciation Month. We will spend the month sharing with you all of the awesome things that animals have meant to our orphanage and the boys in general.

We will have a couple of blogs by animal lovers who have agreed to contribute. Since the introduction of animals here at the orphanage, they have become a massive part of our daily life.

Last month was Health Awareness Month. We had a great guest blog by Dr. Stephen Renfrow. Thank you for bearing with us as we establish this awareness month concept. We did not post as many blogs as we anticipated because I had a health scare myself and was out of action for a couple of weeks. Life happens.

You may wonder why we need so many animals. The first reason is straightforward: sustainability. We survive on the donations of kind folks like yourself. Most of the contributions come when people read our blogs, feel a connection, and are compelled to help us meet our needs. But the truth is, we do not get very many donations outside of designated projects like this. There are months when we have very little in our general budget and have to make tough choices. We pride ourselves on integrity, so when someone donates to a specific project, 100% of their money goes to that project. PERIOD. It is not held in case we come up short with our general budget. When we do come up short, first and foremost, our priority is food for the children. When there is a deficit, they still eat a healthy, well-balanced diet like usual. Next in line is their health, then comes school, and on down the line. The truth is that some months we come up a little short in paying salary, school fees, hygiene, budget, or whatever is last in line.

The animals are a way for us to be self-sufficient here in the case of months where the funding is lacking. Our goal is to sell chickens, eggs, and milk from the water buffalos and goats and meat from goats. This will help us to provide extraordinary care for these precious boys. Our ultimate goal is to be sufficient one day. We have the desire to take in and care for 150 boys in total. That means an increase of 110 more boys. I don't like thinking about how it will be to provide for 150 when we can barely feed forty some months, but there is hope.

By adding animals, we will be able to naturally increase our numbers and provide them with everything they need to grow, learn, and live.

The second reason we want so many animals is that after we are sustainable, we want to be a blessing for other orphanages. No Longer Orphans is the sole supporter of the

Shiloh Orphanage, but we also want to help others when and where we can. We have a network of over 100 orphanages with almost 10,000 children. Many of them do not even have enough resources to provide healthy daily food requirements. We know some orphanages who feed only rice to their children for every meal. We want to be part of the solution. We can donate some of the offspring to other orphanages by breeding the purchased animals. We plan to hatch thousands of chickens every year to give to different orphanages and at-risk women to help provide eggs and meat for their children.

Those are the two main reasons we want to purchase the animals we have listed. Our goal is to be sustainable within five years through this animal initiative. Your donation of any amount is multiplied exponentially. Your gift of a chicken is multiplied when you factor in that the chickens we raise will lay about 500 eggs in their lifetime. If we were to take just 10% of those eggs, hatch them, and continue to do so, your donation of one chicken could potentially be a donation of 5,000 chickens within a few years.

Here is the breakdown of what the current cost of each animal is.

* baby chicks: $.25 each
* Four-week-old chicks: $1 each
* Ducks: $5 each
* 1 Water buffalo with calf: $800
* Geese: $20 each
* Guinea Fowl $5 each
* 1 Goat: $100

Please prayerfully consider helping us purchase new animals.

Andrew M. Lepper

We have a project fund called The Love Project. You can make a donation at https://www.nolongerorphans.org/love-project and designate it for animals

Chapter 10

At the Playground

We have given toys and gifts to the boys through the years, but we don't have many everyday things they can play with. We always have cricket bats and balls as well as soccer balls to play with, and there is usually a daily game of some sort. But we have not had a playground of our own. Our next best option was to visit our local park and use their playground. We have done this a few times, and we all have a lot of fun. We pack a lunch and load up on the bus. We buy snacks and sodas on the way. It usually takes us about 15-20 minutes to get there, but we sing the whole way. Once we arrive, we make a beeline for their playground equipment. They have monkey bars, swings, slides, and everything you imagine a good old fashioned playground having. We usually wear ourselves out before sitting on benches or under a nearby tree to eat lunch. After lunch, the younger boys will go right back to the playground while the older boys will play a pickup game of soccer. Our boys always play hard. So it is not as safe for the smaller boys. None of our boys are overly competitive; they never play to win at all costs. But they are intense and only know one speed- full blast. So the younger boys hang back and prefer the playground when we are at the park.

It got me to thinking. When we are home, and the younger boys hang back, what do they play? They are very inventive and come up with some crazy made up games, but I wanted something more.

So, for Christmas last year, our goal was to build a starter playground for the younger boys to enjoy. It would also have swings for all ages to enjoy. We were quickly able to fundraise the money and sought to buy a playground and have it set by Christmas. But things are not so easy in India. It took us a long time even to find a reputable dealer. There are zero big box stores in India, like so many people are accustomed to. I couldn't just go 10 minutes down the street and buy a kit. Things here have to be ordered from overseas. And then the waiting begins.

We contacted many companies, but most never showed up to access our needs or space. Finally, in early February, we found the right man. And he even had a catalog! We picked out exactly what we wanted and waited three weeks for it to be shipped to him. Once he got it, it rained for a solid week, and he was unable to install it. Finally, once he did install it, we realized that it was missing quite a few parts. So he ordered them, and we again started the waiting period. This time it didn't take as long because we urged him to drive to Delhi and pick up the missing pieces.

On March 20, 2016, we finally had the ribbon-cutting ceremony for our new playground. The boys were excited. They each had a part in cutting the ribbon to inaugurate it. Our playground consists of 3 regular swings, one baby/toddler swing, two slides, a platform, a seesaw, merry go round, and spring horse. Our goal is to add to it every year.

Not a day goes by, where almost all of our boys do not use some part of the playground. It has become the gathering place for free time, and now the boys even use it as a place to play cricket and soccer. Thank you so much to the ones who helped to fund our playground. It has been significantly used, and we truly appreciate your gift.

Chapter 11

Baptismal Pool

Sometimes you cannot give your kids what they want. Sometimes you struggle to provide them with what they need. It's a hard road and tough balance providing either sometimes.

Last summer was a real struggle for us. There were so many trials that we were going through that we were just being crushed from all sides. It was one of those feelings where it had gotten so bad that you thought that nothing could make it worse.

I cannot go into the details, but we were burdened. The boys felt it too. Kids can sense the stress their parents are under. No matter how hard we try, they still can sense it. Sometimes they feel like the cause. Sometimes they go out of their way to help relieve some of that stress from us. Knowing that my boys can sense my anxiety is almost more stressful than the actual pressure. Does that make sense?

We had some tough times, but I just wanted the boys to feel like kids. They are not the source of our problems, and the more that we can help them realize that, the better. We try to do little outings here and there like going to the park or eating out occasionally. But in the heat of the summer, it's hard to muster enough energy to do that.

When our building was constructed, they built a baptismal pool right outside our kitchen door. To the untrained eye, it just looks like an open concrete water storage tank. No water pipe is leading into it, and there is no drainage. But steps are leading down. It's meant for baptisms. (Also it says so on the blueprints.)

When we reach our boiling point, I commission the boys to scrub the inside of the tank. They use bleach and brushes and make it sparkle. They know that this is just the precursor to a day in the water. After they have done their cleaning, we fill the water to about 3 feet. The tank itself is roughly 6 feet wide, 12 feet long and 6 feet deep. So adding 3 feet of water is a lot of water. But it is enough once you add 40 kids in there. The water level rises to what we like.

There are no pumps. There are no filters. There are only 40 sweaty, stinky boys jumping, dunking, and having the time of their life. I always get in with them, but only at the beginning. It doesn't take long before the pristine water becomes a murky brown. But the boys don't care. They play and play and play until their heart is content. And that is our intention.

I have approached a few places in our city that have swimming pools. I wanted to rent it out for any price so our boys could swim. I asked people to name their price. But no one will even give the boys a chance. Once they hear that the boys are from

We Are Shiloh: Stories of the Shiloh Children's Home

our children's home, the pool owners refuse. They do not want any dirty children in their pool. This is sad but true.

It truly doesn't matter. Our boys are valued and have value. Who needs to go to a hotel pool? We have our very own. We have a pool where we don't have to worry about etiquette. We don't have to worry about how clean or dirty we are. We just have to worry about having the most fun possible. And THAT is what it is all about!

We Are Shiloh: Stories of the Shiloh Children's Home

Chapter 12

We Grow Grass

This chapter is not meant to be a double entendre even though I know it looks that way. I am not trying to be tongue in cheek when I say we grow grass.

Farmers for centuries have let their animals graze on grassy fields. We do not have that option to devote to letting the animals graze like that. Partly because we don't have a huge farm and we need to use our fields for staple crops like wheat, corn, and mustard. We don't let the animals free range all day because our field is very deep.

If we were to let our goats graze in the back section, we believe people would jump the wall and steal our animals before we had the chance to run back there. Of course, no one is taking a 1200 pound water buffalo, but there are still people in our area that would rather us close up shop than care for the boys. I wouldn't want someone to kill or poison our water buffalos when they were out of our site. It has happened before.

We try to stay on top of things. Our original two water buffalos disappeared during our prayer time one night. Things happen.

So all that to say that we grow our grass for the animals. We give the animals a lot more than grass, so a whole field dedicated to pasture is not needed. For our buffaloes, we feed them bajra stalks that have been ground up into chaff. We mix that with the grass we grow and add mustard oil. We cook it over an open fire outside to make it a bit more digestible. It may seem strange, but it's what they do around here.

The grass is an important part of their diet. The chaff is the equivalent to dried hay. The mustard oil helps the mothers produce more milk.

But we don't just give grass to the water buffaloes. Our goats and chickens also love it. Goats will eat anything, but they love the grass. And there is nothing better this side of heaven than an egg that has been laid by a grass-fed chicken. It is out of this world.

The grass we grow is known locally as berseem. In English, it is known as Egyptian clover. Our animals love it. We plant an acre of it at a time. We have that acre split into seven sections. Each day we go to a section of that field and hand-cut all the berseem down to about 2 inches above the ground. This provides plenty of grass for all the animals. The next day we move to the next section of the field and repeat. By the time we get back to the first section the following week, it has grown back enough to give the same amount of grass. And the cycle continues.

When we first decided to grow our farm and get animals, I knew that I didn't want to bring in a lot of animal feed from the outside. I wanted to grow as much feed as possible. It not only saves money, but it makes money. Take, for instance, the wheat we grow. If I fed 1 kilogram of wheat to our animals, I would get eight times more money from the sale of milk and eggs than if I had just sold that 1 kg of wheat in the market. This is our strategy.

We grow our grass for multiple reasons- it is more healthy, cost-effective, and generates more money for us. We love our animals, and we love that we can grow our grass to feed them.

We Are Shiloh: Stories of the Shiloh Children's Home

Chapter 13

Fire Biscuits

S'mores- that childhood classic. No childhood would be complete without the experience of sitting around a campfire roasting marshmallows. Couple with being able to put the gooey marshmallows between two graham crackers and top it off with chocolate, and you have a little bit of heaven.

The last time I was in the US, my friend Melinda Stembridge asked me if there were something she could do that would be a little different for the boys than what they are used to. Melinda and I have been friends since high school. Off the top of my head, I quickly said S'mores. Not sure where the thought came from, but that was what I was thinking. So Melinda sent me a huge Amazon box filled with marshmallows, Hershey's candy bars, and graham crackers. This box was huge. It was so big I had to do some calculations and leave part of it behind. I didn't have enough room in my suitcase for 30 pounds of S'mores. But I was able to pack enough for everyone in our home to eat at least two.

When I arrived home, I told the boys that I had a surprise for them. I told them that we would build a massive fire and make cookies. I waited for them to finish their evening prayer. As I waited, I stacked enough wood to build a small house in the form of a bonfire. This was going to be a significant fire. I put cardboard boxes at the very bottom, and I was ready to go.

I assembled the boys outside once the sun went down, and we started the fire. It was blazing hot in no time. I instructed the boys to get thin, sturdy sticks that we could use in the fire. We don't have enough coat hangers to use for the marshmallow rods, unfortunately. The boys misunderstood me because they all ran back with their perfect sticks and began throwing them in the fire. I told them not to throw them in the fire again, and they ran off to get new sticks.

Once they had the sticks, I gave them each a piece of marshmallow and told them to roast it. I ran inside and began to assemble the chocolate atop the graham crackers. They were soon done with their marshmallows and began to line up in the doorway as we helped them construct their S'mores. They had a blast. Everyone loved it. We had enough ingredients, so we went ahead with round two.

All of the boys had a blast, and even the staff had an excellent time. The best line of the night was when one of the smallest boys approached me. I asked him if he had a good time. His response was, "Oh yes, Papa. I am excited for the next time that we can make "Fire Biscuits." And there you have it. The next time you enjoy a S'more, think about our boys and the fun they had eating fire biscuits.

Chapter 14

Shiloh the Protector

In case you didn't know, we have a dog at our home. It doesn't seem like a dog that you would expect to find in India. When most people think of India, one of the main things they think of is the heat. Our city was at one time the hottest recorded city in India. It was once 126 degrees in our city. So you probably would not guess that our dog would be a Saint Bernard. Who was the genius that decided to breed Western Alp mountain dogs in such a hot place? In December 2015, Susan told me that we had the chance to "adopt" this puppy. I had no desire for another dog. At the time, we had Yoshi. He was the Yorkshire Terrier that we adopted in 2006, and that had been with us since then. When Susan officially moved to India, Yoshi moved with her. He was the only "child" we had in the US. So I had no desire to add another dog. Especially one that was extremely hairy and could grow up to a whopping 260 pounds!!! But I started thinking about the life this puppy would have. Would someone adopt him and give him as much love as our boys and staff could? With his heavy coat and thick hair, would he have a home that was cool enough for him? When I started thinking of him more as what he needed rather than how it would affect me, I quickly agreed to adopt him. We have rooms with fans and guest rooms with AC, where he could stay when it was overwhelmingly hot. Every square inch of our 30,000 square feet of flooring is marble, so I knew it would be cool for him. We also have a lot of lands for him to run. We came to find out that he was born in September, right around the same time as Micah. So we just decided to give them the same birthday. We officially adopted the dog at Christmas of 2015. When we brought him home, all of our boys fell in love with him immediately. I asked them to name him. They told me they would think and give an answer later. After two days, I thought they had forgotten. I had also asked all of our supporters on Facebook, and I had some good options in case the boys forgot. When I asked, they told me that they had given it a lot of thought and had even voted behind closed doors. The boy's spokesman told me, "Papa, we know this is the Shiloh home. We know that we are the Shiloh boys. But we want to name the puppy Shiloh also because he is the protector of our home. He will keep us safe. He will be a friend to us." And with that, we named our St Bernard puppy Shiloh. Shiloh, the dog, has been one of our home's main fixtures since the day we brought him home. He has grown from a somewhat small ball of fur to a strapping dog with a bark that bellows and reverberates through our 30-foot ceiling like a shout at the grand canyon. This is not the kind of dog that sneaks up on you. His shadow alone strikes fear in me at times. You hear him long before you see him. We have had visitors that have locked themselves in rooms or jumped on the roof of our van just because they heard him bark. The funniest time was when someone locked themselves in his 8x8 dog pen because they couldn't reach the van's roof in time. Shiloh has become our protector. Its as if he knows what his duty is. He takes this responsibility seriously. But he is also gentle. If you take the

We Are Shiloh: Stories of the Shiloh Children's Home

time to get to know him, then he becomes your best friend. He will overwhelm you with his size as he rubs against you, seeking your affection. Thankfully he is not a jumper because that might harm more people than its worth. I have observed him over the last three years. He has learned the boys' voices, their laughs, and even their shadows. I am serious. I have seen him bound out of our room because he heard a voice in the dark of night only to realize that the shadow is that of one of our boys. He immediately stops barking and greets them with affection. I have seen him in a room of 50 children approach the new ones and examine them because they are new. They are scared to death, but Shiloh wants to make sure you are safe for his family. If Shiloh deems you as safe, then you have a friend for life. You have a friend who will watch your back and protect you in any circumstance. I have seen him "protect" our staff and even church members from what he deems unsafe. Shiloh is an amazingly loyal dog. He has wedged his way into our bedroom. He is now our house dog and sleeps on the floor unless he is needed. If we need him, then he always comes running. There is one specific story about Shiloh that I want to share. One morning we had our staff prayer. Shiloh was with us, resting at my feet. One of the staff members noticed that a dog ran across the front entrance of our building. Stray dogs have always been a problem for us. They have killed hundreds of our chickens through the years. Once a dog gets the taste of blood, it will kill until it is stopped. So when we saw this dog, we all leaped into action to chase it away. A few of the staff ran through the front doors while at the same time, I ran out the back door. In case the dog ran to the back, I wanted to cut it off. Shiloh followed me barking even though he didn't know exactly what was happening. As soon as I reached the back door, I knew we had a problem. I saw a dead chicken just to the left. I followed that around and found another dead chicken. I kept running towards the front to meet up with either the stray dog or the staff members. When I had almost reached the staff, I found one more dead chicken for a total of three. By this time, the staff had cornered the dog between the corner of our wall and our smaller wheat field. This whole time Shiloh had been trying to figure out what the problem was. We had trained Shiloh to have no interest in the chickens. We had never had a problem with him being around them. On this day, he didn't even bat an eye as we passed the three dead chickens. He did stop to smell them, but it seemed as he was trying to solve a case as he examined them. But the moment Shiloh saw this cornered stray dog, he transformed. I had never seen him that way. He took off running and was up to speed in no time. He was running so fast it seemed that he covered 20 yards in just three bounces. As we were all trying to figure out what to do with the stray, Shiloh reached him. Shiloh fought with him for a second and somehow grabbed hold of the stray dog's throat. Shiloh began to whip the dog around violently until it was soon dead. We were all standing in shock. We had seen Shiloh protect us before, but we had never seen him act this way. For lack of a better word, it was primal. I was proud of him because of how he ran into harm's way, trying to protect the chickens and us. But what he did next was what surprised me. With the dog still dangling from his jaws, Shiloh began to march towards the back of our building. We had no idea what he was doing. When he reached the first dead chicken, he loosened his clinch, and the dog fell. Shiloh straddled over his lifeless body and began to growl at him. Not a soft, slow grumbling growl, but a growl that said, "You messed with my chickens and my people. This is what you get." I watched dumbfounded as Shiloh again picked the dog up and carried him to the second dead chicken where he dropped him and repeated the vicious growl. He did this again for the third chicken. He grabbed the dead dog for the last time and carried it to our trash pile, where he dropped it and walked back to my side. He sat on his haunches, looking in the direction of the dog. Maybe it's just my way of over-explaining it, but as Shiloh sat by me, he almost had an air about him of a King looking over his kingdom. He had vanquished a foe and was reveling in the glory of a battle well fought and won. I have never been more proud of that dog as I was at that moment. Please don't think I am glorifying the death of that dog. If I had my way, the dogs would never come on our property to begin with. This way, they can roam around wherever they want and live a long life. But when you cross our property line and kill the things that feed my family, that's when you become my enemy. We don't have chicken because they are fun. We have them because they feed my family. Shiloh knows this also. He knows that his job is to protect us, our animals, and our land. Most days can be boring here with nothing special going on. But on those few days where outsiders or trespassers threaten our livestock come over to take what doesn't belong to them, I know who I can trust to help. I can trust Shiloh. He is the best dog a man could ask for. He protects my children, staff, and family. He is equal parts warrior and confidant. He is not just a man's best friend. He is Shiloh... The Protector.

An update: Shiloh got sick and started having organ failure. Here is the post I uploaded the day he died:

September 23, 2019. Shiloh the Protector died this morning. We are broken-hearted. We buried him by our gate as a reminder of what he meant to us. His grave is facing our gate as a reminder that he was always on the watch for us. I am firmly convinced that he deterred a lot of bad things from happening to us. Please pray for Micah and the boys because we have lost our pet and our friend. RIP Shiloh. You were a great dog.

Section 3: The Boys

Chapter 15

I Hate Math: Addition and Subtraction

I'm not too fond of math. I have never been. Just ask Clayton King. He says math is of the devil. He says that "God is not the author of confusion. Math is confusing; therefore, if math is confusing, and God didn't create it, it must be of the devil." He has a point.

Actually, I love addition and multiplication. I'm not too fond of subtraction or division, or any of the rest of it.

This is what I mean: For the summer, we had three boys go home for vacation. I waited patiently for them to return. It just didn't feel the same without them. I honestly could hear three fewer laughs during our playtimes. I felt three fewer hugs every Sunday morning after our worship service was over. Three fewer bodies were running around, and I could feel it in my heart. School started on July 2nd, and they had not returned yet. I was getting worried. On the 4th, I came back from the vegetable market, and they were there sitting under our neem tree. Their mothers were there also. When I saw them, I felt that everything would return to normal, but I was wrong.

Their mothers had decided to remove them from our care and have them back at home. They were coming to withdraw from school and to gather their things. My emotions were so mixed that I still haven't come to grips with them yet. I mean, on one side I was so happy they would be at home with their mothers.

There is no alternative to a mother's love, but I was also profoundly saddened firstly because their mothers are impoverished and have no jobs. What kind of life will my boys have? What will they eat? Secondly, they were being removed from school with no plan to go back. What will become of them? I feared they would continue in the never-ending cycle of poverty, just like their parents and their parents' parents. Education is the only way to break the cycle. I was also distraught because these are my boys.

They call me Papa. Their fathers had either died or ran away, and I stepped in and took the title seriously. I love them as my own. I would willingly give my life for them, and here they are saying goodbye. It's been a month, and I haven't heard from them. Honestly, I don't know if I ever will. God allowed me to have a special bond with them that will never be replaced. I don't want it to. I cry when I remember them. I grieve.

Fast forward to yesterday. I had been in talks with a local

We Are Shiloh: Stories of the Shiloh Children's Home

pastor that knew of three brothers that needed a home. Their parents are destitute and cannot take care of them. I guided the pastor through the paperwork we needed to receive the boys.

Yesterday, the three brothers arrived. It was emotional watching them have to say goodbye to their father. They were confused, dejected, and I can only imagine that they felt abandoned. It wasn't long before the other boys had taken them under their wing. The other boys told them stories about me and assured them that everything would be okay. They sheepishly called me "Papa," even though I am sure they find it a little weird. Today, they hit the ground running, and you would never be able to tell that they haven't been here for years. They are just one of my boys. They are tender-hearted, feisty, and protective of each other, just like me.

So, I lost three boys and gained three boys within a month. I feel a bit like Job. To be honest, I have never fully understood some people's interpretation of what happened to Job. I mean, I know what happened, and I believe it. He lost all of his sons and daughters. Then, in the end, he was given back the same amount of sons and daughters and increased in other ways.

The part that always gets me is that even though he was given seven sons and three daughters in the end, how could it ever replace the heartache of losing the first ten? There is no way it can. If I lose my house, I can build it again. If I lose a child, I will never be the same. Even though Job was "restored," I don't think he ever forgot the first of his children. It is made to seem that he had ten children when in reality, he had twenty. Ten perished, and ten were alive.

Andrew M. Lepper

This is how I feel. My heart is on my sleeve. I am rejoicing that today I have three new sons. But they do not replace three that I lost. They are in addition to the three I lost. Counting the twenty-eight boys we currently have, I am a Papa of thirty-one boys. I will miss you, Ronnie, Asher, and Reuben. I will always be your Papa. My heart is big enough for them all. Soon, we will have one hundred boys, and they are each special, even my three new boys, Thomas, Abel, and Eustace.

Chapter 16

Meet Wally

This is not an easy story to tell, but it needs to be told. For safety reasons, we have changed this boy's name to Walrus, or Wally. Wally is twelve years old. Wally's' father lost his mother in a gambling debt - a card game gone wrong. Reread that last sentence. You didn't read it wrong. I wish this were a fictional story, but it is not.

His father truly lost his mother in a drunken card game. His mother was now indebted to and had to leave with another man. When his father came out of his drunken, high stupor, he realized what he had done. He did the only thing a coward knows how to do. He took it out on Wally. He beat him so severely that he cracked and broke Wally's skull. You read that right. The father beat his own son so severely that HE BROKE HIS SKULL!!!! I am crying just thinking about it.

Wally was knocked unconscious and drifted in and out of consciousness for the next two days. His mother waited two days before she built up enough courage to run away from her new "man." She ran to the police which also brought in social workers. They went to the home and found Wally and his brother. Wally was admitted into the hospital and slipped into a coma for a month. That was honestly the safest place he could be.

After he came to, he, his mother, and his brother stayed at a battered women's shelter, but it was temporary. The police and the social workers brought the two brothers to us. His mother was also there. It was emotional. The boys did not want to leave their mother. The younger brother quickly assimilated and was having fun in no time. But Wally was not happy. After his mother left, he cried uncontrollably and cut his arm. He would have done anything to have his mother come and take him away.

I sat with him and held him. I didn't talk too much, tell him that things were better, or that this was happening for a purpose. I just simply held onto him, and he clung to me. I have an advantage. When new boys come to us, the last thing they want is for someone to replace their mother and father. They have a hard time opening up to the other staff. However, since I am a big white teddy bear figure, most cling to me. They do not see me as a threat to replace their father.

Wally stayed by my side for the first month. It was not a fun month. When I took him to school to be admitted and placed, they informed me that he was previously in eighth grade. He was first in his class and hadn't made a B in two years. When they tested him, because of his brain injury, he couldn't even recite the alphabet. They had no choice but to place him in Kindergarten.

Here was a twelve-year-old boy who had lost his mother; his father had brutally beaten him, had no home, was in a new environment, and was now having to deal with his traumatic brain injury by having to start school ALL OVER AGAIN!

It was not pleasant, to say the least. He felt different, strange, and awkward. He was embarrassed. When he first arrived, I could tell that he was dealing with a head injury. He would stare off into space and be zoned out. Many times, he would say to me that his brain felt like a cloud. This poor boy was facing every uphill battle imaginable.

We simply loved him through it. I am not here to say that he is entirely well. He is not. He is still dealing with abandonment issues. His brother adjusted the moment he arrived, but Wally still feels awkward and out of place. He knows he doesn't think or act like the other boys his age, but he knows that he is loved. He is beginning to adjust and come out of the fog and cloud he has from his PTSD and brain injury. I will continue to be there with him every step of the way, holding him tight, and letting him cling to me. He is still on the way up the hill, but he is doing better. That's what I live for.

You see, this is why we do what we do. We stand in the gap for these precious little boys and young men when the world discards them. We are there to pick them up and protect them when the world abuses and beats them. It's what we are called to do. God has uniquely equipped us for this. It is the essence of who we are. Seeing the small strides as Wally has made in such a short time gives us the resolve to keep fighting. We have added fourteen boys in one month. Many have similar stories to Wally's. Their arrival has destroyed our budget.

We are at the end of our financial rope. These aren't case studies for us. They are not distant stories we have heard. This is real life for us. To see one of these boys rebound the way Wally has makes this whole thing worthwhile. It's a life worth fighting for, even when we don't know where the next support will come. There are countless boys and girls outside of our door with stories like Wally. We don't have the budget to support them, but God does. We firmly believe that if He sends them our way, He will also send the people to partner with us. That makes me feel loved in a way that I try to show the boys.

We took a picture of Wally when he first arrived. If you saw it, you would notice the blank stare and the emotion and hurt behind the eyes. We took another photo one month later. It is of the same boy who now feels loved, secure, and safe. This is what No Longer Orphans does for these boys. Thank you for remembering us in prayer and for considering supporting us as God leads you.

Chapter 17

We Are NOT Orphans

I will not mention names for this story because I do not want to bring unnecessary attention to any team that has visited us. It was just a simple interaction, but it melted my heart.

We had a team visiting us. They had been here for a few days and were still with us when Sunday rolled around. So naturally, they joined us in our morning service. We proceeded with our routine, and then towards the end, we asked the team if they wanted to share a little bit about their trip. One by one, they came to the front and told the boys how much they enjoyed spending time with them. It was an excellent time. Towards the end, someone came to the front and, through translation, told the boys that it was a blessing to be able to visit our orphanage. There was an awkward silence, and then the boys started gently laughing. It made the team member uncomfortable, so they repeated their last sentence, "Thank you for letting us stay at your orphanage." The boys began to laugh even harder. The team member was visibly embarrassed because they were unsure of what they said was so funny. I was sitting in the front next to the person, so they looked at me and asked what they said that was so funny. I looked at the boys and locked eyes with Raphael. I told the team member to ask him what was so funny. They asked what they had said wrong. Raphael's response sent chills down my spine. Honestly, I didn't know why the boys were laughing. I thought maybe something was lost in translation. But our boys are kind and respectful, so I know they didn't intend to shame anyone. Raphael stood up and said, "You told us thank you for letting you stay here at our orphanage. This is not an orphanage. An orphan has no father. We all have a father. He is sitting next to you. This is a children's home. This is Shiloh Children's Home. We are the Shiloh boys, and this is our home. We are trying not to laugh, but it is funny that you tell us in front of our father that we stay in an orphanage." It was like Raphael did a mic drop. I know my mouth dropped. I was stunned. That was one of the sweetest interactions I had ever been a part of. It still gives me chills thinking about it, or as the boys say, "goose pimples." It finally dawned on me that the boys "got it." They knew that we were a family. They knew that we were here for them and that we weren't leaving. I have described many times that we have an orphanage, even though our name is No Longer Orphans. The sole reason is that it is just easier for people to understand what an orphanage is. But no matter what we call it or what name it bears, this is just HOME to my boys. It is not an orphanage or even a "children's" home. It is merely HOME.

Chapter 18

The Pain of Losing

There is a previous chapter entitled "I Hate Math." It told of us suddenly losing three boys only to gain three more in a matter of a few weeks. It is still hard when I imagine the three boys that left us. I still remember their faces.

That was easy compared to what we faced in 2016. In the span of a month, we lost 13 boys. THIRTEEN. They all left for various reasons. Similar to the last time, some went home for the summer and just never returned. A few returned but no longer wanted to be here. We love these boys with everything we have. But part of that love is trying to instill discipline in them that they will not get elsewhere. We have expectations of every boy. First, a home of our size without expectations or discipline would collapse on itself. If we had 40 boys running around with no guidelines, it wouldn't be very pretty. But most importantly, we have disciplines and expectations because we believe our boys can make something of themselves.

Almost all of the boys come from destitute labor families. We have the crazy belief that they can rise above that and be anything they set their mind to. They can be doctors, lawyers, and engineers. They can be artists, musicians, teachers. There is no limit to their dreams. But we put expectations on them because otherwise, dreams would never become a reality.

Having a dream in and of itself leads to nothing. You must act on the dreams and put in the sweat equity to bring dreams into reality. I wish I had a dollar every time I talked to the boys about putting the work in for their dreams. Many times boys have told me that they want to be doctors or engineers. I sit them down and pull out their grades. I ask them how they could get accepted into medical school if they fail math and science. But it doesn't just end with my questioning their studies.

I ask them what I can do to help them get better. We just don't tell them what it takes to excel in school. We provide the means to make it happen. We give them adequate study time and hire tutors to assist them. I am foolish enough to think that even though you may not be naturally gifted, you can work hard to make something happen even if that means working harder at math and science so you can become a doctor.

We believe in our boys, and our expectations show it. But some boys have never had anyone push them to greater things, so they feel uncomfortable. They gravitate towards doing as little as possible, but we expect them to do more. With that said, there is a delicate balance between pushing the children enough and overdoing it and pushing them too hard.

Kids deserve to be kids. They need time to laugh, play, and

explore. We afford them this. This is just part of growing up. But study time is study time, and we expect them to take it seriously.

Because we have so many boys, we have to keep a schedule. We cannot have 50 people living under one roof, keeping 50 different schedules. So we have a time for waking up, prayer, meals, playtime, and study time. It becomes chaotic, very fast if we didn't. Can you imagine a 3rd-grade class where the teacher let the students do what they wanted when they wanted all day long? What would get done? The same principle applies to our schedule.

The boy's families have entrusted us to care for their boys and provide them with an excellent education. And we rise to meet that challenge. But the sad truth is that even though their family expects us to provide this for them, they do not expect much from the boys themselves. When the boys return home, they run amuck. There is no schedule. The boys come and go freely and wander the streets. Their family doesn't feed them as we do here, and most do not care where they are through the day.

When they were home for the summer break, some boys had zero structure or discipline. So when they returned to us, they didn't adjust well. We tried to have as much grace with them as possible, but it didn't matter.

One boy, in particular, began to run away frequently. I cannot disclose full details, but it became almost an everyday thing. He would run through the fields and jump the fence first thing in the morning when the other boys were getting ready.

We would only notice once the boys were loading up on the bus to go to school. We would search around and quickly find him. He told us he just wanted to go home. He had no mother and father, and his grandmother abused him, so we asked him why he wanted to go back so badly. He told us it was because his grandmother lets him do anything he wanted. We asked him about meals. He said she didn't feed him, but he would instead go hungry without rules than to eat healthy food but have to study all the time. So he just kept running away.

This is hard to write. Partly because we fear what people may think of us. But mostly because we are left with a huge void. We keep asking ourselves if we did enough; if we could have done things differently. But we talked at length with all the other boys, and they had different feelings. All of them told us that they loved the discipline because they have never had that before. They said that they love it because it shows them that we care about them. They take pride in their school, their daily duties, and their relationship with us.

The remaining boys were a comfort to us as we dealt with the loss of 13 boys in a month. As mentioned before, some just decided to stay home instead of returning from summer break. A couple ran away, and we had no choice but to force their immediate family to take them back. I cannot go into detail, but they put us in a position of jeopardizing the whole children's home, so we had no choice but to send them back.

There is one story in particular that broke my heart. There was one boy who kept running away. We had been told by the police to get the situation fixed and fast. We asked the boy's father to take him home, but the boy's father refused. We

We Are Shiloh: Stories of the Shiloh Children's Home

then asked the boy's father to sign an affidavit that said that if his son ran away, that we couldn't be held liable (the police demanded this.) The father agreed. But I was not expecting what happened when his father arrived.

His father barely made it through the door before his son ran to his arms. But the father would not embrace him. Instead, he pushed him away. Instead of comforting him, he began to shout at his son. His words were like arrows, piercing the ears and hearts of his nine-year-old son. "Stop it! I didn't come here to take you home! I do not want you! You are not welcome in my home anymore. You need to stay here with this new Papa and Mommy, who love you more than me! Stay with them because I do not want you." And with those last words, the father threw the affidavit in my direction and walked out, never to return.

We still have not seen him. His son was still standing in the doorway, shocked and sobbing uncontrollably. His two older brothers were standing behind me, just as shocked. Until this point, they had not discouraged their brother from running away. Maybe it was because they wanted a little more freedom if their brother left. Perhaps it was because they felt their younger brother would be better off at home. Who knows? But they were indifferent up until that very moment.

As their brother crumbled onto the floor in a sobbing mess, I knelt beside him. I decided not to say anything. I just simply put my arm around him and embraced him. I was as shocked as he was, and that is the only emotion I could muster because I was choking back my tears. We knelt for what seemed like hours. After some time, his brothers came and joined us. I didn't have to say anything. They said it all. They said, "This is our home. This Papa loves us more than anything. Let us be happy with our home here. Let us forget our old life. Mother left, and Father mistreated us. Let us take the love of Papa and Mommy."

And at that moment, this young boy became strengthened. He became resolute. He hugged me like there was no tomorrow. And he moved forward. We have not had a single issue with him since that day. His grades drastically improved. He has become a leader of the younger boys. You can tell that he genuinely feels like he belongs, like he is home. While fully correct, it's not the same story for all the boys. A few have left for various reasons. And we feel the loss. To go from 45 boys to 32 in less than a month leaves a void, both physically and emotionally. We choose to continue to fight. We must fight for the boys that remain.

Not a day goes by where I do not think of the boys that have moved on. I question what we could have done differently. I may never know. I will not lie and say that we have moved on from this. How can we? This affects us. This affects our relationship with the boys who are still here. How could it not? I find myself wanting to withhold emotions and love because I am afraid of getting hurt again. This is just the truth. But I must remember that one day all of the boys will move on. Even in a perfect world, they will go to college; get married; start a family. Would I knowingly withhold the only love the boys receive because I am afraid of being hurt? This past year was the hardest of my life. Mostly because of the loss of boys. But I have rededicated my life to loving freely with no strings attached, even when the love is not returned.

Chapter 19

Manu

Let me tell you about Manu. He is Susan's nephew, the son of her older sister. His father died when he was very young. His mother is uneducated and works for a family in the Middle East.

Manu bounced around from family member to family member his whole life. His life growing up in Kerala did not have much structure or continuity. There were weeks where he stayed at a different place every night in the village.

He never finished school. He is still very immature. But that is because almost no one has ever modeled what it means to be an adult; what is expected of a man. There are not many men in Susan's family, not good ones at least. Her father left the family and died homeless a few years ago. Her uncles are out of the picture. Her grandfather passed away many years ago. Her older sister's husband was not a good man and died also. I came along 14 years ago, and I was the only man in the family until her younger sister got married. All that to say-Manu has never had an adequate role model.

A couple of years ago, he began to be quite a handful to my mother in law and the other families that he stayed with. He was 18 at the time, and he wore his welcome out as fast as he arrived. He had become disrespectful and had no direction. In essence, he came to us because no one else wanted him.

It is not that we hadn't always wanted him, we did. But he is from Kerala, which is about as far away as you can get from us in India. He didn't know Hindi and didn't want to come. But once we realized that we were his last and only chance we quickly begged him to come to us. I had one person ask me, "Why do you want HIM? He will never amount to anything." At that moment, I realized that I would do anything to give Manu a better life. Every kid deserves a chance for a better opportunity.

So we welcomed Manu into our home. In one way, it was a smoother transition because he was already family. But it was equally as tough because he tried pushing our buttons every chance he got. This was partly because he just wasn't raised to show respect to anyone. He just didn't know. Teaching simple things to Manu was like training a chicken to swim.

(I do not know how hard that is, but it has to be near impossible, right?)

When they dropped Manu off, some family members stayed with us for a few days. On the second day, Manu asked for the keys to our old van to wash it. I didn't think anything of it at the time. Within 10 minutes, my mother and law ran in screaming that Manu was driving, and he would kill himself.

I went to see what the fuss was all about. Manu was in our front driveway just driving in big, slow circles. He wasn't causing any harm. I flagged him down and began to talk to him. I asked him who taught him how to drive. He told me that no one had taught him; he had just learned by observing others. I said I was impressed at how well he was driving but scolded him because he didn't take permission to drive around, he only took permission to use the keys to open the door to wash the car.

This quickly became a pattern with Manu. He would do the most fantastic job around the farm, but he did things without asking or even letting anyone else know.

One day I woke up and found that Manu had hand-dug a vast, massive hole in the middle of our field. He had spent ALL night digging it. But it was right in the middle of the area that we were preparing to plant. I asked him what on earth he was doing. He said that he noticed that the water buffaloes needed a better pond, so he just decided to dig one- in the middle of our crop field. This is just how Manu's brain worked. He has a fantastic amount of self-motivation. The problem is he never clears his endeavors with us before he starts acting on them. What Manu lacks in common sense, he makes up for in initiative. He was not happy that I made him fill in the pond that he had just worked so hard to dig. But I told him that had he asked, I would have shown him the spot that I had already marked off to dig a new pond. He was shocked to learn that I had plans to dig a pond.

I told him that this is how people function- through communication. When we adequately communicate with one another, we are all happy, and more can be accomplished.

I wish I could report that things ran smoothly after that, but they didn't, and that is ok. Manu is a work in progress. He had 18 years of poor communication. Eighteen years of no direction and people not having much belief in him. We desire to guide him, and we have great confidence in what he will do in this life. But it takes time for him to believe in himself and to know that we believe also.

I admit that I am extra hard on Manu. That is because time is precious, and we are trying to get him prepared faster than anyone else. If we cannot instill some simple life lessons in him soon, we may not have the chance later. These life lessons include time management, discipline, teamwork, maturity, and so much more. Notice that I didn't say hard work. Manu is one of the hardest working people I have ever met. My father would be proud of him.

When Manu first came, I asked him what he wanted to do with his life. He responded that he wanted to be a driver. I can get behind that. That is a noble profession. Manu didn't have much male mentorship in his life, but it didn't take me long to figure out that most of the men that he looked up to in Kerala were drivers. So I affirmed his choice and set out to figure out how we can help him. Being able to get a license is not the same as being mature enough to drive a car. We are still dealing with Manu's maturity issues because he has never had responsibility for his whole life and has been treated like a small child. He is of driving age but not mature enough to drive yet, in my opinion.

One of the ways I wanted to teach responsibility and maturity was through our farm. I gave Manu full responsibility for our chickens. He became responsible for feeding, watering, shelter, gathering eggs, and cleaning up their area. He is in charge of selling the eggs and butchering the chickens when someone needs it.

Manu is an extremely hard worker but couple that with his supernatural stubbornness, and we have interesting encounters. I am sure there are days that he thinks I am Satan himself. I try to show grace to him when needed, but I am tough on him because I love him enough to do so.

I will only say that even including our staff; I am the person with the most faith in Manu. I know he will be a great man one day. There are days when he is the most immature in our building, including the small boys.

But as I write this I think back in the two years he has been with us. I reflect on where he was when he came to us-unwanted, uncared for, no discipline, very immature, and no direction to get where he wanted to go. All he knew is that he wanted to be a driver. He had no clue how to get there, and no one to help him.

But we cannot concentrate on where we came. Or even where we are. We must focus on who we should become. We are all works in progress. Manu is a work in progress. We worship a God of second chances. He never leaves us in our past sin or dwells on it. God patiently looks to who we can become, who we should become. God's patient love never gives up. That is my desire for Manu.

I know that one day it will be said of Manu- "That man was an orphan, but now he has a successful transportation company (or whatever else he does). He was an orphan, but now he drives for Kings." But my prayer for Manu most importantly is this, "Once he was an unwanted orphan, but now he is a Godly man who loves his family and gives glory to God. he once had no direction but now is a leader for many."

Chapter 20

Dinosaur Uncle

We have a boy named Raj. This kid is amazing. He is ten years old. He reminds me a lot of myself when I was his age. He is compassionate but forgetful. Caring, but a little ADD.

One day he got on the bus and wasn't wearing his shoes. He honestly didn't realize that he wasn't wearing shoes because he likes to go barefoot around the home anyway. He searched and searched and couldn't find his shoes. The bus left without him. After a few hours of looking, he finally found his shoes in his book bag. He looked at me, and you could tell that he just remembered putting them there. He told me that he didn't want to wear the shoes on the bus, so he put them in his book bag and was going to put them on once he got there. He is so forgetful.

But man is he a boy after my own heart. He is messy, forgetful, and mischievous. Recently the boys drain clogged in their bathroom. The pipes are enormous, so we couldn't figure out what had caused it. A couple of boys came to Susan and confided in her that Raj had stuffed some toys down the drain. When asked why he did it, he replied that he wanted to see if they could swim.

He is also tenderhearted. One day I was hanging out with some boys, and they were calling Raj by a nickname I hadn't heard him called before. They were calling him Dinosaur Uncle. I had no idea why. I asked the boys why they called him such a weird name. They told me it was because Raj liked to keep all kinds of animals under his bed. He was like the guy in the Jurassic Park movie, so they called him Dinosaur Uncle. I told them they must be mistaken because Raj would never keep anything under his bed. They told me to look with them. Raj had a big sheepish grin on his face when he realized that I was about to discover what he had hidden.

Usually, the boys keep all their belongings under their beds in their metal footlockers. Some will keep soccer and cricket balls also. Raj didn't have any of that. He had put his footlocker with his clothes under someone else bed. Under his bed was a menagerie of animals. He had his own little zoo going on. He could have charged admission from the village kids.

Under his bed were clear bottles with an ant farm, other bugs, a baby bird in a shoebox, a lizard, a frog, and an injured ground squirrel. You read that right. He was keeping a full-grown squirrel under his bed. You have to love this kid. He was a little embarrassed and scared that I would remove it all. But I bent down and told him that it was okay as long as he helped the animals live. Don't kill or harm any animal, I told him.

I also told him that I wouldn't tell Mommy if he didn't. So far, she hasn't found out about Raj's zoo. And she doesn't know the true meaning behind why we call him Dinosaur Uncle.

Chapter 21

Welcome to the Family

One day I found Joshua staring at a bodybuilding magazine. He read all the articles, saw all the pictures, and was convinced that he wanted to have a bodybuilder body. He begged me to buy him protein powder and supplements like those that filled the magazine pages. I had some protein powder already, so I gave it to him and taught him how to make a shake.

A couple of weeks passed, and I asked him about his goal. He told me that he was taking the shakes daily, but he didn't see a change. I asked him how much time he was spending lifting weights, and he told me he wasn't lifting at all. I looked at him like he was crazy. If you want to be a bodybuilder, you must BUILD your BODY. He told me that he wanted to be the first bodybuilder ever that didn't lift weights or exercise. I said that that is not how life works. You will not see results if you do not put in the work.

Caring ABOUT something is not the same as caring FOR something. If you care for something, then your life reflects it. Almost everyone cares ABOUT orphans. I mean, you would have to be a pretty miserable person not to care about the needy or at risk. But do we care FOR orphans? God did not call us only to have a regard for orphans, not just positive thoughts or good vibes. He never asked us to only pray for the orphan. He called us to go; to visit, to love, to weep, to supply.

We have a fantastic group of friends who do just that. They not only devote their prayers for our boys, but they stand in the gap financially. They send letters and videos to the boys. They provide Christmas, birthdays, and daily survival.

We are not obsessed with money. Never have been, never will be. We do not desire great and outrageous donations. We yearn for relationships to grow with our partners. We have settled on a motto for No Longer Orphans- WELCOME TO THE FAMILY. This is important to us for two reasons. First, when we take these boys in, we welcome them to our family. For some boys, we are the only family they have. Second, when we partner with you, we also welcome you into our family.

I am sincere when I say that we don't want people just financially to support us. We want you to become our family. Donors will come and go. But we need a family to lean on during good times and bad.

We have people visit us all the time. Maybe you, the reader, can visit us soon. I always tell everyone when they come that the first night they are our guests. But the second night you are family. And because you are our family, money is never a factor. We have never charged anyone to stay with us. We will give you the best we have to offer. A warm bed, a hot shower, a good meal, and fellowship. If we visited you, would you not do the same? If I stayed with you, how much would you charge me for the night? Of course, nothing because you invited me to your home.

Likewise, when people visit us, they are not visiting an orphanage. And honestly, it is not even a children's home. More than anything, this is a family home. We have love enough to welcome as many people as possible into our family. The boys need love, and we need the shoulder to lean on. So I encourage you to not just care about our boys. Join us and care for our boys. We need you. Welcome to the Family!

Chapter 22

Five New boys

I have always said that we are willing to take in every possible child. While this has remained true, we have never actively looked for orphaned or abandoned children. They are brought to us by pastors, family, or police who know that we take great care of our children. Many have asked what happens if someone brings us a girl. We never turn anyone away, but we can't legally house girls, so we refer them to one of our sister homes. We have only legally been able to take in boys. At our height, we had 47 boys. At this stage, the boys were coming faster than our support. But God never allowed a single child to go hungry even for one meal. But this still was a source of tension for me. When boys would arrive at the back of my mind, I would wonder how we would feed them. I wondered where the support would come for them to go to school. How would we provide clothes for them since they showed up with just the clothes on their backs? I am sure they could sense my stress. Here these boys are, in the middle of the hardest day of their lives, and I am standing there, welcoming them with apprehension. They would stand before me having everyone they know abandon them to the point that we were their only option at that moment. I would stand there with my heart heavy to not only welcome them in but also with the unknown of how we would financially care for them. I know they could sense my tension level. This tension at their arrival began to wear me down. I felt horrible that I even felt that way.

One morning I sat on the floor and just prayed. I didn't sing a song. I didn't read a verse. I just sat there and prayed. God had met every one of our needs, so why was I so stressed with the arrival of a new boy? I couldn't take it anymore. I told God that I trusted Him for the needs of the boys, the needs of the staff, and my family's needs. I was done stressing. In fact, we would not go looking for kids unless He told us to. I told him that it was all in His mighty hands. He was the only one that would send boys to us. This way, when boys arrived, it would no longer be a source of tension, but of joy. I no longer wondered how we would care for them. My first thought was to praise God that He sent the boys to us at this time. Their arrival no longer sent me into a spreadsheet tizzy, looking at the bottom lines. I began to look at EVERY new boy in the eyes and tell them, "God sent you here. God will take care of you." I had always known this, but once I put my belief into action, my stress level lessened. To this day, one of the first things I pray every moment is "God; You know our needs. Send us who You will. If someone comes today, it is because You sent them. If a boy comes, we will welcome him with the love of Christ. If someone comes with any other need, I will know that You sent them. Put a hedge of protection around us. We want to give all we have so; please send us only the people you want us to help." With this prayer, we help everyone who comes to us knowing the Almighty God sent them to us for such a time as this.

We added five new boys this year. One was from South India. For safety, we will call him Bruce. He had developmental issues which some people view as a curse here. He had never been a part of a loving family. His mother and father were not together. No one wanted to care for him. Someone reached out to Susan and asked if we could take him in. Of course, our answer was yes. We knew that God wanted him to come to us. Bruce didn't adjust very well at first to our boys. He didn't know how to act in social situations. He would often be in the middle of playing and snap. He would run to Susan crying and would fabricate what had happened. All of our boys are amazing because they gave Bruce a chance to adjust and didn't hold it against him that he would lash out at times. They took it as a challenge to try to make him feel welcome, and many went out of their way daily to include him in what they were doing. Things are not perfect. They never are. It didn't happen overnight, but soon Bruce was more comfortable and melted into his role as one of the boys. We still have tough days, but he has come a long way.

Another boy who came was the nephew of a staff member. We will call him Jordan. He had family situations that prompted him to join us. His uncle and aunt didn't have space in their one-room apartment, so he slept with all the other boys in their big room. Jordan fit in immediately. You could tell that he was "raised right." He had been taught to be respectful and considerate. He was a diligent student and a loyal friend. Within a week, it was impossible to tell that he had just arrived. He was a born leader and was soon leading the smaller boys in their studies and prayer time. Even though he had his aunt, uncle, and cousins there, he loved spending time with all the boys. He just fit in. That is the thing that teams experience when they visit us. It is virtually impossible to detect who are the staff children and who my boys are. My staff loves our boys like their own. And I also love their children as my own. I love the boys in our home the same way that I love Joshua and Micah. No one can tell whose kids belong to who. Isn't that the way it should be?

Lastly, last year, we added three brothers. Their story is not typical. These boys had it rough. They were one of 12 children born to the poorest of parents. Their parents were laborers. Out of the 12 children, these boys were the last and youngest. Their parents were in their 60s. Let's call the boys Charles, Parker, and Ralph. Charles was 10, Parker 8, and Ralph was 6 when they came to us. Their parents lived in our state, although it was the extreme corner, which meant it was almost a day to travel by train. The boys, though, came to us from South India. Their parents had sent their children to the four corners of India to whatever home would take them in. These three boys were at the Southernmost edge of India. They were in a home and doing ok. They had each other to lean on. But the children home there was not as safe as people thought. The leaders of the home were arrested for physically and sexually abusing the children in their care. I don't have all of the details of the home. I don't know how many children were there. All I know is that when the police raided the children's home, all of the children's families came to collect them within 24 hours, except for our three boys. No one was there to pick them up. No one could find their parents. Their parents didn't even own a phone. They finally tracked down one of their older brothers and told him to come to get them. So their older brother made the travel arrangements and set out on a 3-day journey by train. Somewhere along the way, he contacted us and told us the situation. We told him we would gladly take in the boys. When the brother arrived in South India, he found out that his brothers were in jail. You read that correctly. They were in prison. The police had nowhere else to house them, so they had them at the local jail. They were in the same place as the children's home staff who were locked up for abuse. Talk about traumatic. I cannot imagine what these three boys had endured. By the time their brother had reached them, they had spent one full week in lockup waiting. Their brother collected them, and they made the 3-day journey to us by train. Once there they came to us by bus. We met them at the door and wholeheartedly welcomed them. They were terrified. They were crying and scared to death. At this point, we didn't know the full story. I videoed the conversation with their brother on my phone. I focused on them. Later I realized how traumatic this must have been. 2 weeks before, there were in a home where there was reported widespread physical, sexual, and mental abuse. Then they get rescued only to spend the next seven days with their oppressors behind bars. Then their brother, who they hadn't seen in years, shows up to take them home. They spend three days on a train with him only to get off and within an hour have a fat white guy hugging on them and sticking a phone in their face to film them. Of course, I didn't know all of this at the time, but it helped me realize why they were so standoffish. Within three days of them arriving, I had to make a trip to the United States. These boys were at the top of my prayers. I prayed for their little hearts to be healed. I prayed for their minds to be mended. I prayed that we would not come on too strong and just what they needed at any given moment.

Because they came towards the end of the school semester, we had to keep them at home for a few weeks while we waited. We wanted them to take this time to be kids. We wanted them to run and play, ride bikes, scooters, and waste time on our playground. They didn't need to be burdened with school at that moment. But it was tough for them. During that trip to the US Susan called me one day. She said that these three new boys were stuck to her like glue. They went everywhere she went. She had shooed them out earlier that morning to play on the playground. But when she walked out of our room, the boys were sitting in the hallway. They begged her, "Mommy, please tell us what to do. We will clean or help you cook. Just tell us what to do." She told them that she didn't need help with any of that. All she wanted was for them to be little boys. She asked them, "Why do you want to help me so badly? Why do you not want to play?" Charles replied, "We like it here. You don't beat us. We don't want to leave. Please do not send us back. We will do anything you want us to do." She started crying and held each one of them. She told them that we would never send them away. This was now their home for as long as God wanted them to be here.

Some years we have added upwards of 12 boys. Boys have come and gone because of graduating or family struggles. But they will always be my boys; all of them. This year we only added 5. But that was enough. That is what God, in all His sovereignty, decided to give us. We had Jordan, who assimilated faster than anyone we have ever had. Bruce came to us and needed longer than most to adjust. And we ended the year adding Charles, Parker, and Ralph. All of the boys had very different stories. But all of their lives mirror what happens when we begin a relationship with God. It no longer matters what we were before. What matters is that we are now a member of a family that will last for eternity. Without discounting their history, what matters in these five boys' lives is not as much as who they were but what they are now. They are Shiloh boys. They are my boys. And they are now part of our family. We will stand with them through thick and thin. That's what true family does.

Section 4:
Celebrations

Chapter 23

Untold Story of the Best Birthday Party Ever

This is the full story of the now-famous birthday party for the Shiloh Children's Home. It was a very typical Wednesday. I was sitting on a broken bunk bed that serves as a bench on our front porch. I had about twelve to fifteen boys all around me. Some were bouncing balls. Some were relaxing. A few were looking over my shoulder as I looked at photos on my phone.

One boy, I don't remember who asked me when my birthday was. I told him November 7 and asked him for his birth date. He had no clue. I then asked every boy, and no one knew their birthday. I was dumbfounded. I, of course, have all of their records that have their birth dates and personal info on them, but it never occurred to me that they didn't know the actual dates.

They were amused at my reaction. I pushed further and asked

if they ever had a birthday party. The boys had no clue what I was talking about. In India, it is a custom for a person to give other people gifts on their birthday. Many times, people from the community had visited our boys and passed out sweet treats in celebration of their birthday. Not only had none of the boys had their own birthday party, but they sat in amazement as I shared what birthday parties were and recalled some of my favorite childhood birthday party memories.

All in a moment, I looked at the boys and told them, "Guess what! Everyone's birthday is this coming Saturday, and we are going to have a party!" The boys went crazy! They were so happy.

Everyone gathered around, and we planned out what kind of party they wanted to have. Since it is customary in India to give gifts on your birthday, I had each of them draw the name of another boy to give a gift. When each one had a name, I jotted down the gift they wanted to give. Some chose to give a ball. Some a kite. Others pencils and pens. We planned out the party to have cake and ice cream.

For the rest of the week, the boys were excited, but they had no idea what I had in store for them. When Saturday came, the boys left for school, and I headed into town to buy supplies, gifts, food, and decorations. I had it all organized and prepared for when they arrived at 1 p.m. I wanted them to be center stage, so I allowed them to decorate it as they chose. We lacked in decorations, so it was mainly decorated with Christmas lights and holiday-themed decorations. When they were done, it was time to begin.

I made them all sit on the floor. In India, it is customary to give a strand of garland to a person of respect that visits you. It is an honor to receive this garland of flowers. Think of it as a Hawaiian lei. It is full of roses and smells fantastic. Every church and orphanage I have visited through the years has bestowed this flower garland on me. I wanted to convey to the boys that this was their day, and the party was in their honor. I had them come, one by one, as we put the garland around their neck and also gave them a party hat.

Next, we had them come up to get a kite, then brought out the cake. No one had ever blown out candles, so I had an individual candle for each boy, and they came up, one by one, to blow out their candle. They loved this!

Next, I surprised them by giving them the TV they had been asking for over a year. It was candy apple red and awesome! After the TV, I acted like the party was over and walked away. However, I simply walked to my room and gathered the individual gift bags for them. In each bag were a new pair of shoes, a ball, pens and pencils, candy, and a few other items. They were so proud of the shoes that they refused to wear them for weeks. They were giddy, but I told them that the night was just getting started.

Next, we cleared all the gifts and turned the sitting area into a dance floor. We danced like crazy for over an hour and had a blast. They took the flowers from the leis and threw them in the air over and over and over.

When the dancing was through, I introduced them to Bruce Lee. You've already read the blog post about Saturday nights with Bruce Lee. As they sat and enjoyed the movie, I had them come and get the snack tray I assembled. It had quite a few different items, including namkeen, popcorn, and samosas. After the movie time was over, we all slept like babies. Happy babies. The smile on their faces the next day was well worth it.

It may not seem like much of a party, but I only spent about $10 on each boy, including the TV—no big deal. Imagine being in the shoes of one of the boys! You have been abandoned by everyone close to you. Your day is filled with a schedule that has little to no variation. But for one day, you are treated like a king. The joy on their faces made it one of the top days of my life. It proved to the boys that they are valuable, that their lives are worth something, and that there are people who genuinely care and love them. I wouldn't trade that for anything in the world.

A shout out goes to all of the families and friends who recorded birthday videos for the boys or left sweet notes on my wall. A big thank you also goes out to Dr. Stephen Renfrow and all the others who also saw value in a birthday party and helped make it possible. Thank you so much. Just imagine how Christmas will be :)

Chapter 24

Simply Having a
Wonderful Christmastime

So here is the official story about Christmas. As some of you may have read on the Facebook page, I acquired a Santa Claus costume. I didn't even need to buy padding to go inside to recreate Nick's bowl full of jelly. :) Here in India, Santa Claus is named Christmas Father. I wanted to have the most fun possible without commercializing Christmas or taking away from the celebration of Christ.

I decided to let their interaction with the Christmas Father be one of fun and innocence, and not tied up in gift-giving. We had a bunch of gifts for them like balls and cricket bats, art supplies, toiletries, and various other knickknack toys along with their big presents- three different sized bikes for them to enjoy and share. We set everything up on our main stage and had the boys locked in their two rooms. I dressed as Santa Claus, and the fun began. They honestly didn't expect to see Santa. Most had never seen him. The original lore of Saint Nicholas told of someone who came in the night and filled your shoes with fruit and candy, so I tried to keep it simple. I decided to give them each a Santa hat and a piece of candy from Santa. That way, they could have fun and not tie their memory to a gift.

I was a little worried that they would know it was me. I mean, how many 280-pound white dudes are walking around an obscure village in India? As I entered the room, it was apparent that most were just in awe. I disguised my voice and told them that their PAPA was at the train station picking up a guest. I even asked most of the boys what their name was to cover my tracks. I overheard one boy say, "That is not Papa, Papa knows my name." That made me beam from ear to ear. I do know his name :)

I passed out the hats and the candy and danced with each room as we sang Christmas carols. We locked them back in their rooms, and I dashed off to my room to change back into my clothes. Within seconds I rushed back to their rooms and burst through the door, screaming, "Where is he???? Where is Christmas Father??? I was at the train station, and I rushed back as fast as I could!!!"

The look on their faces at that moment was priceless. They proceeded to tell me how much fun they had singing and dancing with Christmas Father. They said he was fun, but he didn't know any names. After their reenactments of what I was already a part of, I made them all line up at the door ready to go out and see their presents just like me and all my cousins used to do at my Grandmother's house for many years. My cousins and I would line up in front of Grandmother's bathroom, making sure we didn't step on the metal grate that covered up the furnace in the floor. We wanted so badly to stand closer to the living room door but knew that the furnace cover would give us a burning we would never forget. I remembered this as I made the boys line up. The boys had no idea what was waiting for them. Not a single boy has ever owned a bike, and only about seven of them have ever even been on a bike. When they walked out to see what was there, you would have thought each one of them had won the lottery. They barely looked at their individual prizes at first. They were all line up to ride the bikes. There was a small bike, a medium bike, and a large bike. We mostly have little to medium boys, so that line was super long. Vikas is one of our small boys, but he couldn't wait. He jumped on the biggest bike and took it around. The funny thing is that his feet didn't even reach the pedals, so he pedaled with one foot and kept going around and around. What a sight! The pictures and video tell it better than I can.

This was the night of December 23. On the 24th, we had a Christmas service on our campus, and around 1,000 people from all over our area came out. I was only able to speak for ten minutes before JP and I had to catch a train to Kota. The train ride seemed to take forever, and we finally reached Kota at 2 a.m. The next morning, we awoke early to enjoy Christmas day celebrations with 600 orphans at our sister home and another 1,000 people from the community. I didn't like being away from the boys, but I had to speak, and I had a really good time. After the service, the ministry did something really fun and helpful. They designated fifty families from the community to give Christmas gifts to those who had a need. They passed out cookware, sewing machines, and bicycles. The neat thing was that the ministry asked local business people and guests to stand up and donate the items.

One by one, the guests went on stage and gave money for the gifts and personally donated items to the families as they came up. I didn't want to be left out of the fun, so I gave two sewing machines in Susan's honor to two older ladies who needed it.

What a wonderful Christmas time it was! I got to celebrate with the boys, sing festive songs, dress up as Santa, speak about Jesus, and give gifts to those in need. Thank you so much for all of you that pray for us. We truly live day to day and are only able to make it by the grace of God. He gets the glory for everything that is given. Thank you so much for remembering us in prayer.

Now on to the New Year! We are grateful to the ones who donated these things, but more importantly, we give thanks to God because we know He heard our cries and He answered us... with manna.

Chapter 25

Birthdays Are Special

Do you remember the details of a particular birthday party? I am sure most of us do. No one remembers their first birthday, but I am sure a lot of others stand out. For me, two birthdays rise above the rest.

The first was my thirteenth birthday. We were rather poor at the time, and the presents were scarce. That is not my favorite thing, although I do remember getting one gift. The game was on the original Nintendo and was called Sky Shark. It was one of the best gifts ever! I played it for hours on end. The game retrospectively looks pretty bland and bad, but at the time, the game was awesome. My favorite memory of that day, though, was being with my family.

We went out to eat at a 50's themed diner in Valdosta, Georgia before going to see the theatrical classic, "Look Who's Talking." The time spent with my family was a memory I will never forget.

The other birthday I remember like it was yesterday was my sixteenth. I had been saving up for months to buy a truck.

I gave all the money I had saved to my dad and told him to surprise me...and he did. He took the money and bought a 1980 Chevy Scottsdale long bed truck. He painted it midnight black and put a pretty decent stereo system in it. I stayed in that truck overnight, just sitting there listening to my favorite CDs. I still remember the way it smelled...like new paint and old vinyl seats. It smelled like it was MINE! I will never forget that day or the gift of the "Black Stallion."

For our boys at Shiloh, birthdays were never a big thing. None of the boys ever had a party, and most didn't even know their birthdate. Well, not until August 10, 2013. That was the day we had a celebration birthday party like never before. Every boy was celebrated. This was the Best Birthday Party Ever.

We will continue to do that. I am working hard on helping the boys realize their individuality. That is hard in a country of one billion people. However, assisting each boy in realizing their value to me, and more importantly, to God, is crucial.

We celebrate every boy's birthday like they are the King of the Castle. My little routine is to take them with me at around 6 pm on their birthday. We drive around for a few minutes on the motorcycle and head to a shop to buy a new change of clothes. They love trying on new jeans and shirt, and they love wearing them home. I also buy them something fun and impractical like a cricket bat, toy car, or soccer ball. Then, we go out to eat at the only fast food joint in our city. It is vegetarian, and choices are a little different, but we have a blast. We eat pizza, fries, veggie burgers, and drink Pepsi.

I remember Ronnie's day. He is ordinarily boisterous, curious, and full of nervous energy. As we sat and ate our fries, he was quiet, and his face was stone cold. I asked him what his favorite restaurant was, and he stared back blankly. I asked him how many times he had eaten out, and he looked around the room and then said, "just now." He had never been out to eat before. He wasn't scared; he was soaking it all in. When we got back to the orphanage, I could hear him telling every boy of the awesome adventure he had.

You see, his birthday was the first one we celebrated this year. On our way back to the home, we stopped and bought a cake for us all to enjoy, complete with his name on it. As we sang "Happy Birthday" to him, he truly got tears in his eyes as he looked at me. I knew how special he felt. This has been told to me verbally by every boy now in their own way. One of our boys, Peter, usually is super quiet. He is active but isn't verbal. He just soaks it all in. After he and I ate for his birthday, we rode around for a few minutes before heading home. As we hit an open section of the highway, I gunned my motorcycle just a bit and yelled, "wooooooo." At that moment, Peter reached his arms around me, gave me a huge bear hug, and said, "Papa, I love this. I am so happy."

These are some of the things I think we take for granted in life. I am not suggesting that you take your birthdays for granted, but we assume everyone has the chance to be royalty for a day like we do. That's all I want for my boys - just a day they can know that I supremely love them for who they are as individuals, that they matter, and that their life has a purpose. As we close out each boy's birthday, there is a time of simple ceremony. We light their cake, sing "Happy Birthday" to them in a crazy Indian key, and blow out their candles.

In India, it is a custom for each person on their birthday to give gifts to others. For every boy, I give them a huge bag of candy to share with their classmates and teacher. Why should they not have that joy simply because they live at an orphanage? Another tradition is for the birthday boy to cut his cake and pass out a piece to every person in attendance. Our boys do this, but before they do, they always feed me the very first piece.

I cry every time. What a sign of humility to give your first piece away to your father. Shortly after they feed me, I take a piece and playfully shove it in their face, in their ears, or down their chest. What is a good birthday cake worth if it can't be smeared on your loved one?

The boys' birthdays are glorious days. It is a day for each of them to give simple gifts to their peers and elders. It is a day for me to celebrate their life with some time of fellowship and laughter, and it is a time for all of us to gather in prayer for the life of that boy and pray that he will be blessed in his coming year. I pray that one day, when he is my age, he will look back on his birthdays, just like I do, with fondness and memories he will never forget.

Chapter 26

Birthday Bread 8-22-14

We just celebrated the 2nd annual Best Birthday Party Ever! It was amazing. Please understand that we are in a constant battle between spending money on what is absolutely necessary and occasionally spending money to establish memories for these boys. Although it may sound controversial, birthday parties are not a necessity of life; however, the memories created are priceless. Our budget was virtually nothing for the party. We used old decorations. I bought the boys an inexpensive DVD player and put their current TV in a box to make it look bigger. They either didn't notice or didn't care. They were just happy to have a party.

It took me days to plan and coordinate, and hours to decorate. Bear in mind that we only have a few staff members, and they didn't quite get the idea when I shared it with them. They thought it was a waste of resources. I mean, we have so many things to do, why spend it on a party? Truthfully, the actual party didn't cost a lot, and I bought the gifts from my pocket. Their gift bags included a new pair of shoes and a new shirt. Have you ever bought shoes and shirts for thirty-six boys in one fell swoop? That was intense. I gave the boys marbles and kites also. The total cost of the kite and marbles was five cents per boy.

I bought a few collective sporting items for everyone to share, like a couple of soccer balls, cricket bats, and a small basketball hoop.

One of the weirdest gifts I have ever given was a loaf of bread. A couple of weeks ago, a local businessman came by and provided a meal for the boys. In the end, he gave them ten rupees each to use at their school canteen. The next day, about half of the boys brought me their ten rupees and asked if I would buy them a loaf of bread each. Ten rupees is about sixteen cents. I laughed.

Trust me, these boys eat good food, but if that's what they want to spend their money on, I have no problem with it. So, I went out and bought the bread. They all shared it and thoroughly enjoyed it. When I was thinking of good things to add to their birthday bag, I immediately thought of the bread. So, I bought forty loaves of bread and added them to the bags. The funny thing is that when I was passing out their bags to them, the thought of getting bread made them giddy. They grabbed the bread and dropped the rest of the things. They didn't even look at what color shoes they got or the style of their new shirt. They were just so excited to get bread! It reminds me of children who get expensive toys and end up playing with the box on Christmas morning. What a hoot!

As I was running around like a crazy person just minutes before the party, a mother brought her two sons to be admitted. She had all the paperwork. I paused what I was doing and gave her my full attention. The two boys were a bit terrified. Knowing that the colossal party was just minutes away, and we had no clue they were coming, we rushed out to buy shoes and shirts and make them a part of the party. The oldest boy was visibly shaken and didn't want his mother to leave; both of the boys automatically knew that this is a home of love. They both embraced me and gave me looks that they knew we would take great care of them.

They immediately called me Papa and seemed to loosen up. I insisted on their mother staying for the start of the party, where we blew out the candles on the cake. This is where every boy gets a candle to blow out. For some reason, I bought two cakes, but it all was soon about to make sense. As a staff member talked to the mother, we found out that it was the oldest boy's birthday.

What amazing timing! He never had a birthday party before, and he just walked into the greatest birthday party ever, and I had an extra cake! Before we even started the party, I had him come up, and we sang "Happy Birthday" as he blew out the candle.

After the gifts were given, we all danced and sang to Bollywood music and had a blast. We then played all the sports and ate the snack trays I had assembled with six different goodies. We had a fantastic time. I cannot compare it to last year because that was a once in a lifetime event. After doing a headcount, we discovered that almost half of our current boys have come since last year. They experienced something like that for the first time, and that's what makes it so special.

A staff member came up to me during the party and told me that this was one of the greatest things he had ever seen. He said he was sorry for thinking it was a waste of money. He told me that money could not buy happiness, but this party made the boys the happiest he had seen. Bread seems to have the power to do that to my boys :)

Chapter 27

My 38th Birthday

The boys have surprised me by taking me out to dinner at a restaurant with a discotheque in the basement. Good times.

Some funny sentences from the forty birthday cards from the boys:

"Papa, I hope that you are thirty-eight years old."

"God gave you a good life."

"God blessy."

"I pary for you."

"Papa, one story for you called Jingle Bells. Dashing through the snow on a one horse open sleigh." (he then writes out the whole song)

"Good bless you Papa"

"May God give you everlasting life"

"Happy Papa, birthday"

*One boy colored me fourteen pictures

*All the Christmas cards sent last year have seemed to have been recycled.

*One boy took a blank Christmas card and wrote his name inside with nothing else.

*One boy glued my business card to the outside of his card.

I am just overwhelmed. These boys are so creative, and they try their best. God does have a sense of humor, and I think He allows me to have some of these funny moments to keep me energized. I genuinely believe the boys value my birthday because I value their birthday. Last night, I went out with Sanjay for his birthday, and he was the happiest kid alive. No one could have wiped the smile off his face. None of them had ever experienced that kind of joy before. I am doing nothing special, merely doing for them what my family did for me - having a day when you are special and treated like a king, a day where "it's your day, it's your way."

Of course, this isn't uncommon for India, but it is unheard of for poor street orphans that were struggling to get by just a few short months ago. I value my birthday not for myself, but for the growth and joy that I see present in my forty sons.

Chapter 28

Christmas Bikes for the Boys 1-7-15

In the unforgettable words of the one and only Pee-Wee Herman, "What's missing from this picture?? It's just me without my bike!!!"

Do you remember the Christmas when you got your first bike? You had a feeling that you could take on the world. Nothing could stop you. The joy and excitement of that Christmas is one you will never, ever forget. You have the opportunity to give the same gift of excitement by donating.

I question the authenticity of a childhood that didn't involve a bike. Well, not really, but bicycles at their essence scream, "childhood memories." I remember one time on Arrowhead Drive, where my friends and I made a makeshift ramp, and we jumped it until the sun went down every day. It was all fun and games when we had a brick as the height. However, the day I removed the brick and added a cinder block, everything changed.

I hit the ramp at full speed and was propelled a lot farther than I had calculated, which sent me over the handlebars when I touched down. I still have scars over thirty years later. Good times, good times.

Or the time that we lived by Long Pond in Lake Park and my mother worked extra shifts for a month to buy me a new bike. We were pretty poor at the time, and I wasn't expecting it. I loved that bike. It was my first bike with gears. We moved shortly after that, and I started a new school within walking distance of our house. I drove my bike to school one day and forgot to lock it when I went for band practice. It was stolen. I felt horrible that I hadn't locked it and felt even worse when I thought about all those hours my mother worked to get me that bike.

That story isn't meant to leave a bad taste in your mouth. I am sure we all have some bike stories from our childhood. It's just a part of growing up.

The joys of bicycles are not lost on Indian kids, and surely not my orphan boys. They know what pleasures lie in the ownership of a bike. At their school, roughly 200 children ride their bikes to school daily (I wish we still did that in the United States). They see the freedom and joy on their friends' faces and want to feel that also.

Last year for Christmas, I bought three bikes for the orphanage. One was meant to do local errands. It was bulky and had a huge basket on the front. The second one was for the older boys. I was wrong in thinking that only the older boys would want to ride it.

They ALL wanted to ride it, and everyone tried. The very

We Are Shiloh: Stories of the Shiloh Children's Home

small kids couldn't reach, but for the medium-sized kids, their feet just fit. "Zachary" was a little on the small size, but that didn't stop him. Although both of his feet didn't fit, one of his feet could reach the pedal at its highest point, so he would ride it one-footed and kick off with all his might when that pedal rolled around.

Even today, when there is daily free time, about ten boys are patiently waiting their turn to ride our single bike. I want this Christmas to be a little different. My desire and goal are to provide an opportunity for every boy to take ownership of their own bike, including maintenance. If there are needed repairs, the boys will be required to pay for them from their canteen money.

First, we need to buy bikes. Won't you help? The cost of each bike is forty-four dollars. We need a total of forty bikes. Please take a moment to change the childhood of an orphan boy today.

NOTE: The follow-up blog post: If you follow us on Facebook, you may have seen our Secret Santa Bike Challenge's fulfillment. It was an overwhelming success! It was a fantastic day that we would not soon forget. The children were amazed and overwhelmed to get such a wonderful gift. They had no clue that they would each get a bike!

On December 23, "Santa" showed up, danced with the children, sang songs before he passed out candy, and disappeared into the night. An hour later, the boys were given what they thought was their only Christmas gift. We gave them a steel footlocker filled with clothes, small toys, snacks, and candy.

They had no clue that this wasn't their gift, but merely their "stocking."

It is our personal tradition here at Shiloh that we give no gifts on Christmas Day. I want that day to be a day of reflection and concentrating on the reason for the season. So, on December 26, it was time. We waited until the boys were having morning prayer, and we wheeled all forty bikes out into the main hall.

After everything was set up, we encouraged the boys to finish their time and see what was in store. The boys flooded out of the room and had differing but awesome reactions. Some stood in awe with their mouths gaping open. Some boys rushed to the bicycles like their pants were on fire. Some boys rushed over to me and hugged me with all their might shouting, "Thank you, Papa!!" It was an amazing time, and the boys continue to enjoy their bikes thoroughly.

Chapter 29

WWE

Anyone who knows me knows that I am the biggest wrestling fan. I remember, as a small child, my grandmother watching Wahoo McDaniel and Chief Jay Strongbow. I was a massive fan of the NWA. I loved the original Four Horseman, Dusty Rhodes, and Sting. But my favorite wrestler of all time was Ric Flair. WOOOOOOO! I remember watching the first Wrestlemania and every one since then. But I wasn't the biggest WWF fan growing up. I loved NWA and USWA, but my favorite was WCW (previously NWA). For me, this was where the big boys played. Of course, I still tuned into WWF because, more than anything, I was a wrestling fan. In the '90s, WWF changed names to WWE, and they bought out WCW. Wrestling has always been fluid. Wrestlers are independent contractors, so they jumped from company to company when their contracts expired. So it wasn't hard for me to start watching WWE once WCW ceased to exist.

You would think that being in India would make it more challenging to watch and follow wrestling. But it is quite the contrary. This country loves wrestling. Multiple sports channels cover it. Wrestling is shown numerous times a day every day of the week. The Pay Per Views are shown for free. The only downside is that if you want to watch it in real-time, you have to get up very early because of the time change. I am glad I have DVR because I am not getting up at 5:30 AM to watch wrestling.

On one of the wrestling programs, they advertised that WWE would be coming to Delhi in January. It was the first time in 14 years that they would be here. In the US, I can see live events as much as I want. And I did. Within 4 hours of my house, there would be some live wrestling at least once a month. My buddy Willy Lopez and I have been to a ton of live events. Somewhere along the way, we added Kenny, and we all go together now. But I have never been to an event in India and thought it would be amazing.

As soon as the tickets were available I bought 3. One was for me, one was for my brother in law Tijoy, and one was for my best friend JP. Soon after, I discovered that the dates would not work for Tijoy because he is a nurse in Mumbai and couldn't make the trip just for the event. So I decided that I would make the WWE trip available for one boy to earn. JP said he wasn't too interested, so I decided to make the third ticket available to a staff member. I didn't know how to make it equitable. How do you choose one boy out of 45 for such a big treat? I wanted to take them all, but at this point, the tickets were sold out for the night I was going. I decided that we would have a Bible memorization challenge. The winner would get the ticket. The same was true for the staff ticket.

I gathered the boys together and told them about the trip. I told them that the winners of the ticket would have to memorize a particular passage from the Bible. Most kids were not interested, but six boys and two staff decided to take the challenge.

For the memorization, I told the boys to pick either ONE of James chapter 1 or Matthew chapter 6. I told them to memorize as much as they could. I didn't want to choose a set amount of verses. How could I pick a boy if all of them memorized the same amount? I told them just to memorize as much as they could, and the boy that memorized the most would get to go.

Boy, did they take me seriously. They were studying and memorizing every possible moment they had. I gave them just five days for the challenge. On the day it was time to pick a winner, we gathered all of the boys together, including the nonparticipants. I wanted all of the boys to see the hard work that the challengers had put in. I told the rest of the boys that they were going to be the judge. I gave them all clipboards and told them to grade the participants on a scale of 1-10 based on how much they had memorized and how well they did. Since the boys only had Hindi Bibles, I had Susan and JP there to monitor their speech.

I called the six boys and two staff forward. I told them that the competition was about to begin. I wanted to know who chose which book, so I asked the boys who decided to memorize parts of James 1. All 8 raised their hand. This confused me. Why did they ALL choose to learn James, and no one wanted to memorize Matthew. So I asked them. I said, "No one wanted to memorize Matthew 6?" One boy spoke up, "Papa, we memorized that also." Let me get this straight- every boy was so interested in the competition, and they all wanted to win so badly that they memorized everything possible. They had all memorized 61 verses in 5 short days. They still attended school and did all their chores. And they still found the time to memorize 61 verses. It was truly amazing.

I already had a lump in my throat, thinking that I had only two available tickets for eight people who had worked so hard. We sat and listened to all 8 recite the 61 verses. This took ALOT longer than we were expecting. We had planned for it to be just a few minutes, but it took almost 3 hours. Some of the boys needed some casual help when they stumbled. They needed us to feed the first word of a verse here and there. One boy stood there confident and recited the 61 verses word for word and did so in blazing fashion. He repeated the whole thing in less time than it took most boys to read 15 verses. As they would recite, the rest of the boys were giving scores and taking notes.

When all was said and done, I had eight people who had worked their tails off, but I only had tickets for 2 of them. I felt bad. I didn't know what to do. I didn't sleep well that night, wondering how I could fix the situation. Could some of the boys that didn't win at least ride with us and stay on the bus when we went inside the arena? That didn't seem fair.

The following morning Susan and Micah headed off to the Delhi airport to fly to South India. Until that point, Micah had not met his Indian grandmother. I went along for the ride to keep them company. Remember that the tickets for the event were sold out. I had a dilemma on my hands. I had told the boys that I would announce the winner when I returned. Susan and I talked about the tough choice. We even discussed not going at all because it just didn't seem fair. She suggested that I look up the tickets one more time online. SO I did. It appeared that there was one remote location in Delhi that had seven tickets left. That is precisely what I needed. 8 people had taken the challenge plus me made it 9. I already had three tickets, so I needed six more. I dropped Susan and Micah off at the airport and hightailed it to the ticket venue. On the website, it was listed as CCD ticket sales. I made my way to where I thought it should be but couldn't find the location. All I could see was a coffee shop. I asked around, and no one knew what I was talking about. About that time, a worker came out of the coffee shop and asked if I wanted tickets to the WWE event. He wasn't a worker at the coffee shop; he was the worker for the ticket venue. Whew. I had found him. I asked him why it said CCD Ticket Sales on the website. He said that it stood for Cafe Coffee Day, the coffee shop that I was at. His company had a partnership with the coffee company for a remote location.

I thought he would escort me to a side office to do the transaction. Instead, he guided me to a table in a corner where he had his laptop set up. There was someone already sitting at the table purchasing tickets. I sat close by and waited for the previous customer to finish. I was so tense because the website said there were only seven tickets left, and I needed 6. How many would the guy in front of me need? When the time came, he told the ticket worker that guy he needed two tickets. My heart sunk. The worker wanted to confirm that he needed two tickets, so he asked the customer again. The customer surprisingly said that he needed to confirm first with his friend. I was on pins and needles. The customer called his friend but quickly hung up. He said, "My friend cannot make it for that night, so can I just buy one ticket?" I felt like giving him a big kiss right on the cheek. Before long, his transaction was done, and I sat across from the ticket worker. "How many tickets do you need?" I confidently replied, "I want all that you have!" His response was, "Wow, five tickets? That is great." "5 tickets?!?!?! That is all you have?" He told me that he would look again. He squinted his eyes and then took out his reading glasses. As he put them on, he said, "Sorry. You want six tickets?" I about had a heart attack right there in that Cafe Coffee Day. "Yes," I said. "But hurry. We can talk about other stuff later. Just sell me the six tickets before it is too late." And he did. And with that, I had the six tickets I needed to make the trip complete. I quickly made my way back home. The 3 hours seemed like 30 minutes because I was so excited to hand out the tickets.

Remember that the boys didn't know where I went. They thought I went to the airport. In their mind, I was announcing two winners, a boy and a staff member. Even the staff didn't know.

I gathered the boys together and tried to make it as dramatic as possible. You would have thought that I was ready the paternity results on an episode of Maury Povich. I started with the lowest scores. "Ricky, with a score of 7.5, you did an outstanding job. But you will NOT be going to WWE!" Even though one by one, the boys' faces filled with sadness, I was having too much fun knowing that they would all be redeemed in the end. One by one, I got down to the final two boys. They thought that only one would win. "Zachary, with a score of 9.5, YOU are the winner. YOU will be going with me to watch wrestling!!!!" All of the boys were so excited for him.

Of course, they all wanted to go, but they all genuinely care for one another and were happy that he was the winner. I told them that I would announce the staff behind closed doors. The two staff members were there and were confused as to why I didn't do it then. I then turned and walked out of the prayer room, leaving all the boys a little shocked. I stopped just in the hallway where no one could see me, but close enough to hear them. There was positive but confused chatter. "I thought my score would be higher." "I wish I had a second chance to do better." I let them simmer for a moment. Not because I was trying to rub it in, but mainly because I wanted them to savor it more when I made the bigger reveal.

I walked back into the room and told them I had an announcement to make. I said to them that I had looked at the score sheets and I had made a mistake. "The winner is not the only one who is going. Everyone is going! Including both staff members." You would have thought they won the lottery. They were so excited. They were screaming and jumping around. They kept saying over and over, "Thank you, Papa!" I was just blessed by all of their hard work and dedication. I will gladly spend every penny I have for them to work like that.

A few days later, the 9 of us loaded into a small van. It was pretty packed, but we were elated. We sang songs all the way to Delhi. The driver wasn't as friendly and was noncompliant for most of it. He wasn't too happy that we were so lively. I begged him a few times to stop somewhere to eat, but he was more interested in getting us to the venue. I was too blessed to get stressed, so I didn't want to make a big deal about it. I knew that there would be something to eat at the arena.

When we arrived at the arena, we took about 200 photos. There was a long walk to the front doors after they let you into the main gates. But there were life-size posters of all the wrestlers, so we took turns getting our picture taken with them. We made it to the front, and there was a Dominoes tent at the front entrance. They told us that we could buy pizza but that we couldn't carry it inside. We didn't mind. All 9 of us got personal pan pizzas and Cokes. We all talked about what we might see inside. I was the only one with any event knowledge, so it was both funny and exciting to hear what the boys predicted. One boy thought that a wrestler would personally escort us to our seats. One boy thought that I knew all the wrestlers, and I could take them backstage for a meet and greet. I had contacted WWE many times via email and the internet, begging them to let our boys come backstage. But I never got a reply. It is ok. The boys didn't know and still had an excellent time. One boy said that when he went to the bathroom, he thought a wrestler might be in the stall and waited for him to come out. They had creative ideas about what to expect.

We made it to our seats, and the show began. I am not going to give a full detailed report because that is not what the trip was about. The lighting was horrible; the sound was worse. The whole atmosphere was nothing like what I am used to in the US. But that didn't matter. I was enjoying something special with my boys. They had worked hard to earn it, and they were having the time of their lives. We were unable to buy souvenirs because they hadn't expected a big turnout and had not adequately prepared. They had sold out before the show was over. All the boys slept like Mac Trucks on the way home, pooped after such a fantastic time.

After we had made it back home, I reflected on the whole experience. We indeed had the time of our lives. But more important than that was what it took the boys to get there. They had memorized 61 verses. The Bible says the Word of God does not go out void. At some point in each of their lives, I believe they will be in a time of crisis. There will come a day where their back is against the wall, and they do not know where to turn. When they turn inward, they will remember the verses they memorized. They will gain strength and courage from God's Word that was planted in their hearts so long ago. And that is what this was about for me. Because one day, they will not remember much about the trip. They will not remember the wrestlers or the others that went with them. But they will not forget the verses tattooed on their hearts. For me, I would pay everything to make this happen. A ticket to a wrestling event is nothing compared to God's Word that has pierced their minds. To me, it is worth it.

One final part of the story I would like to mention. A couple of months after wrestling, we had another memorization challenge. This time we were taking the boys to an arcade with bowling and cricket batting cages. We told the boys that everyone who met the challenge would be able to go. We set the bar a little higher but still had 15 boys who qualified. We broke the winners up into two trips because we couldn't afford a bus. I noticed on the first team that only one boy had qualified for both the WWE trip and this one. It was Zachary. He was the one who had memorized all of the 61 verses from the first completion word for word and had done it in the fastest time. I asked him to tell the other boys how much fun we had on the first trip. He is not a shy kid, but he responded that he didn't remember. I asked him to at least tell them about his favorite wrestler from the first trip. He said he couldn't remember. I asked him to at least mention the name of one of the wrestlers that we saw. He said he couldn't remember. I asked him to tell them about what we ate before we went in to view the wrestling. He told the other boys that we ate burgers. I reminded him that we didn't eat burgers. We ate pizza. "Oh yeah," I asked him if he could remember anything about that trip, and he just looked at me blankly. I was so confused. Had the trip been nothing that I remembered? After 2 minutes, I asked, "Well, do you at least remember part of the bible verses?" "Oh yes, Papa, I remember it ALL!" And with that, he spent the next few minutes quoting ALL 61 verses verbatim. This was what it was all about. We still do these memorization challenges. We always have fun incentives. Why not? But for me, it is not about where we go or what we do. It is about encouraging the boys to store God's Word in their hearts. And for that, I will pay anything in the world.

Chapter 30

My 41st Birthday Party

Last year was an epic birthday. The boys learned how big 40th birthdays are, and they did not disappoint. They curated an hour and a half long program for me complete with song, dance, and skit. They choreographed every dance and skit and even wrote a song for me. They had a slideshow to the song Good Good Father. They acted out a play of my whole life. It was epic. All had a fun time.

But for my 41st, it was different. There was no fanfare. No one goes crazy for a 41st birthday. But what they did was even better.

They still decorated our Great Room. They again sang me happy birthday. We again ate the nasty Indian birthday cake. (I think it's unpleasant because they always mix rosewater into the icing. No one wants to eat flowery flowers on their cake.) After we enjoyed the cake, I thought it was over. But it was just beginning. They had me sit in a chair in front of our stage. They all sat down in front of me. I was a little apprehensive about what would happen. Would they bring out a pinata? Would someone try to scare me from behind? I had no clue as I sat there.

What they ended up doing has become one of my favorite nights of my entire life. To a person, each one stood up in front of me and then proceeded to tell me what I meant to them. I had boys crying me and telling me that without me, they would have no father. They laughed at all the fun we had through the years. Some staff said similar things and included Susan, Micah, and Joshua in their words. They recounted how they had nowhere to go, but Susan and I took them in and grafted them into our family. Our cook Vimlesh had been raised at an orphanage as a child. She told me that in her life, she had two fathers. One was Dr. MA Thomas. The other was me. This was special to me, even though she is quite older than me.

It was the sweetest time getting to hear the impact you have had on others. Sometimes you never know. You feel like you are giving all you have but wonder if anyone really "gets it." It is also hard because I am like most people and do not do well in the spotlight. I do not handle praise well. But I think of all the people that have impacted my life. I wish I had the same chance to tell them what they mean to me. So I do not want to squash someone else's blessing. I cried with every person and hugged them because they mean as much to me as I do to them.

I want to share one specific story that was shared because it hit me the hardest. Names have been changed for safety. Some of the story cannot be shared, but I will share all I can.

A few years ago, we needed some work done around our building. We had been cheated repeatedly by people in our area that kept charging us too much. We needed to renovate a room that included fixing the broken concrete wall, painting, and rewiring everything. Someone mentioned that there was a worker close to us that was fair. So we called "Doug" to come to give us an estimate. He was a very humble, quiet man. He was thin as a rail. Not a lick of fat on his body. But he worked hard. He got the job done faster than he estimated for less than he quoted. We knew he was a keeper as a worker. We learned that Doug was the village equivalent of a master electrician, so we started using him for everything we needed. One day after a few months, Doug asked Susan what made us different. Why were we happy all the time. What was our motivation? She and another male staff member told them that we were Christians, and because of this, our actions were different than others. It wasn't like he didn't know we were Christians. He was, after all, working in our church this whole time. But Doug sensed we weren't like everyone else, so he inquired. One of our staff spent countless hours with him sharing, and Doug decided to become a Christian. He immediately felt happier. He begged us immediately to go to his house to pray for his wife, who had been dealing with substantial issues. Susan and some staff ladies went and prayed with Doug's wife, "Patty." She also became a Christian. Soon they were at our home multiple times a day eager to learn all about their new life. We then discovered that Doug had severe Tuberculosis and was close to death. He had never shared this with us before. He shared with us that he could no longer afford to buy medicine because once he became a Christian, he was ostracised from his family and the village. No one would hire him. He was ashamed to tell us. So he almost lost his life. As soon as we found out, we all agreed to pay for 100% of his medical needs. Our name is No Longer Orphans for a reason. 1st, we care for orphans who have no father. But 2nd and sometimes, more importantly, we come alongside families to prevent their children from becoming orphans.

When I looked at Doug's three children, I knew we must act to prevent them from having to come to our home. Doug fought through all of the procedures and medicine he needed to survive. We were there with him every step of the way. Today he is in remission. He is an active part of our church. He is grateful for what No Longer Orphans has done for him, and he is thankful for his faith. I share all of this with you as my recollection of Doug and Patty's story. But what they shared with me on my birthday digs a little deeper. I will share it in Paul's own paraphrased words.

"I was sick with Tuberculosis, and no one at Shiloh knew. I had worked for them for a few months, and they were good to me, but I did not tell them about my TB. There came a time when I was so sick that I could not work. But our bills kept coming. I kept getting more sick, and the hospital and medicine bills were more than I could ever pay. One night I told my wife that I couldn't do it anymore. I was sick, tired, and there was no end in sight. I told her that our whole family should take poison and die. I was ashamed because I didn't want to suffer anymore, but I also didn't want my children and wife to suffer because of me. My wife agreed that we should take poison and die. At that moment, I thought of Shiloh and how they were always so caring. They had hope. I told my wife that we should wait until the following day to take the poison. First, I wanted to go to Shiloh and ask them where they got their hope for life. I did this, and they shared with me the love of God. I became a Christian, and I felt better than I ever had

We Are Shiloh: Stories of the Shiloh Children's Home

inside. I asked them to share with my wife, and they came and prayed with her. She also became a Christian that day. We no longer wanted to take our lives because we knew we had people who loved us and a God who loved us. But it didn't get easier overnight. Because I became a Christian, no one would hire me. I kept getting sicker because I was still ashamed to ask the people at Shiloh for help. But I knew I didn't want to take my own life. I prayed that God would either take my life or make a better way. One night I was so sick I thought I would die. I hadn't been able to pay for medicine in a few weeks, and I thought my life was over. Patty called Susan, and she and Andy rushed over. They prayed for me and loaded me up immediately and carried me to a private hospital. There the doctors told them that I hadn't taken my medicine, and my life was in critical condition. Andy and Susan told my family and me that they would help us out by paying for my medical bills. They paid for every single one and also gave us all the food we needed. They helped pay our bills and were always around praying for us and just spending time with us. They do not know it, but they saved my life. They saved my wife and children's life. We were ready to take poison, but they helped us and showed us God. We are alive because of Andy, Susan, and the Shiloh Family."

I do not share this with you because I want praise. I thought hard about not including the story. But I feel led to share it not because of what we did, but what God did for Doug. We didn't do anything. We were just willing to do what God put on our hearts. What about you? Is there a Doug or Patty in your life? Has God called you to help someone that you don't know their full story? You may just be saving their lives.

Today you can find Doug and Patty at our home various times throughout the day. Patty hangs out with the ladies and does whatever they need help with, even if it is scrubbing the floors or folding laundry. She is always down for times of community and fellowship. Their three children are as much a part of Shiloh as our boys are. For three years they have been included in every celebration we do. When our boys receive anything from the US, so do Doug's kids. We celebrate their birthdays and anniversary. If you didn't know you couldn't pick Doug's kids from our own. As for Doug, there is always something for him to do. Lots of maintenance is needed in a 20,000 square foot building. But Doug's favorite thing is to make pens in our workshop. He helps the boys and enjoys making the pens himself. He is still softspoken and humble, but he has beaten his disease. He is vibrant and always present. I pray that you can meet Doug one day and learn why his testimony made my 41st birthday the greatest one so far.

Section 5:
Special Friends

Chapter 31

Murghi Uncle & David's Guest Post 2-25-15

David Bissette is one of my best friends in the whole world. We have similar tastes in music, movies, and humor. He is a wise grassroots man I sought out many a year ago for his advice on Chunky Junk, a fair-trade jewelry company we own that supports our orphanage. I discovered that we are cut from the same cloth. I think of him as more of a big brother, more so than any friend I have. He has been to Haiti with me doing building projects for an orphanage.

We were even in an epic movie that one will soon not forget. Well, it's hard to forget something you will never see. The movie was a low-budget film that will probably never make the light of day unless you search for it. David is the founder of The Grain Mill of Wake Forest in Wake Forest North Carolina, http://www.grainmill.coop.

The Grain Mill of Wake Forest specializes in bulk foods

and whole grains, natural salts and sweeteners, and baking supplies. He was the first person I called when God moved me to start Resplendent Farms here at the orphanage. Within three weeks, Dave was on a plane over to India. Because he was vital in the startup of our chicken farm, the boys started calling him Murghi Uncle, which in India means Chicken Uncle. He is a true friend in the purest sense of the word. I am deeply indebted to David Bissette. His practical love and respect for animals have taught me a lot. I have asked him to write a guest blog for Animal Awareness Month, and he obliged grandly. I hope you enjoy it as much as I have. Thanks, Dave! - Andy

David Bissette's Blog Post:

Several days before Hurricane David wound a path of destruction and havoc through the eastern coast of the United States in 1979, my dad brought home a small flock of chickens. He told me these were special chickens. Rather than laying plain old white or brown eggs, these "Easter Egg" chickens would lay eggs that were blue or green, and sometimes even pink. I thought it was the coolest thing ever.

As a kid, I learned a lot from keeping chickens. Since I was solely responsible for the upkeep of the birds, I had to ensure that my chickens had fresh water and feed, even on the cold days when their water was frozen solid. Keeping chickens was also my first experience dealing with the sensitive topic of death. Something that my parents didn't explain to me was that there's a reason why everything tastes "just like chicken." It's because everything in the woods seems to enjoy eating them. Raccoons, skunks, snakes, opossums, and the neighbor's dogs all had their eyes on my small flock. One day, I came home from school to find the chicken coop empty. There was nothing there; no hens, no rooster, no feathers. I was completely dumbstruck. I found a very traumatized rooster in a cardboard box in the basement.

Since then, I have had many, many batches of chickens. I learned some valuable lessons from those first birds of mine: kids don't have to be insulated from the way things are. I found out the hard way that chickens are at the bottom of the food pyramid, and death is the natural and inevitable consequence of life.

Additionally, I learned that chicken wire is very good at keeping chickens in, but very bad at keeping dogs out. Thirty-plus years later, the memories of my special chickens is still intact. When Andy Lepper invited me to come to India and Shiloh Orphanage to set up a chicken coop for the boys, I knew I had to do it. One long plane flight and a white-hair inducing cab ride to the city later, Andy, the boys and I were ready to get down to the brass tacks of building a chicken coop with whatever materials we could scrounge.

The first step for the boys was building the enclosure, which was a woven fence made from pieces of old bedpost, and the woody stems from last season's lentil plants. Then the "Murghi Mahal" was constructed of two old bunk beds, a rusted air conditioner cover, some extra scrap lumber, and a piece of donated Lexan roofing from a local business owner. The total cost of building our new chicken palace? Less than five American dollars!

Populating it was even easier. After a jaunt through the nearby village, we found a farmer willing to part ways with a rooster "Bada Lal" and two hens, one of which had chicks. We woke the next morning to the sound of cock-a-doodle-doo coming from outside, a familiar sound from my childhood, and one I've missed greatly since moving to the city.

Unfortunately, by the time our chicken coop was completely populated, it was then time for me to return from whence I came. Andy sent me regular updates on the status of the chickens. I think I was nearly as excited as he was about their first eggs, and heartbroken when one of the chicks drowned during a rainstorm.

What really excited me was that several of the boys had taken a liking to caring for the chickens. One boy, Mannie, had become a right fine chicken whisperer. Then came the day when Andy told me about a new breed of chicken he'd been researching; one that could better withstand the dry summer heat in the city and still put on weight. He told me of his plans to purchase hundreds of these birds and raise them not only for eggs and meat for the boys of Shiloh, but for commerce and barter in the community as well. And lo and behold, if he ain't gone and done it!

The orphanage is a regular working farm now. They even grow and grind their own feed for the birds. I am certainly proud of what's been accomplished at Shiloh, and very grateful that I could be a small part in the much bigger picture of teaching these young men some of the sustaining principles of self-sufficiency and life in general. – David Bissette

Chapter 32

Kanti

In 2015 Kanti came to help Susan personally. Susan had a high-risk pregnancy, so she needed someone to be her hands and feet for times when she was fatigued. Kanti had been a helper with another family in South India, but they were aging fast and no longer needed her.

Kanti was raised at an orphanage, and she has no family. She has no education, no training, and had nowhere else to go. She would have been put on the street had we not taken her in. I do not tell you this to act like we are saints for giving her shelter. Kanti is just one of many girls who are in the same situation. They have no one to care for them, no education, and nowhere to run. They are forced to be helpers in people's homes because they have no alternative.

Even from the beginning, we did not treat Kanti like she was a helper. We treated her like family; as a long lost sister. She wasn't hidden from site, toiling away in our kitchen. She went where Susan went; as a friend and confidant. She got the best accommodations we had to offer, our best guest room. She had more space than any of our other staff along with AC (she didn't want it), a water heater, and the softest bed we could find. Once again, I am not trying to pat ourselves on the back. I wanted to illustrate that we treated her as a guest or an equal more than a servant. She was more of a VIP to me because of the care she was giving Susan during her pregnancy. But she was super shy and standoffish. She had never had much interaction with anyone and was confused when I attempted to carry on conversations with her. I think that was just never done where she previously was. It was more than six months before she even made eye contact with me when we spoke. That was tough for me. I was taught to look someone straight in the eye as a sign of respect when you talked with someone. It meant that you were talking with them, not at them. But I understood that it was not intended as disrespect on her part. She was probably scared to death that I would even interact with her anyway.

Slowly she became part of our family. She began to kid around and joke. More so with Susan, but she was finally opening up. I believe she felt like she finally had a family. From the beginning, Susan wanted more for Kanti than just to be our helper. Even from the beginning, we paid her a salary equal to what we pay our other staff. She was not expecting that and refused to take it. So we kept it in an envelope for her.

Susan's intention from the beginning was to give a better life to Kanti. In case you didn't know, the vast majority of marriages are still arranged here in India. It is not a Hindu thing. It is an Indian thing. Even Christians here arrange marriages. Susan worked for months to find the perfect man for Kanti to marry. After a few months, she found the perfect one. The arrangement, engagement, and marriage is a book in and of itself, but in the fall of 2015, Kanti got married. Her husband is a hard-working man and has been a great provider. We have known him his whole life, and they make the best couple. We gave Kanti's salary that we had been saving plus some extra money as a gift for their wedding and seed money to start their life. She indeed was a blessing, and we were blessed to help her.

It didn't take long before Kanti called us to tell us that she was also pregnant. In India, it is not uncommon for husbands and wives to be away from each other for extended periods of time. This was true for Susan and me as we were separated for the first year of our marriage. Kanti asked us if she could stay with us after she got pregnant. This was not because of her marriage, but more to do with her husband always traveling and working. She didn't want to be alone. She wanted to help us and be close to Susan so she could get advice on her pregnancy. So she moved back in. Susan went with her for all her pregnancy doctor appointments. Kanti was still in the first trimester, so she was still at full speed. She was a huge blessing daily as she became the nanny for Micah. She was around him every waking moment. Even when we encouraged her to rest, she still wanted to hold Micah. I would watch her as she would be looking in Micah's eyes. I couldn't help but think that she was thinking forward to the day she would have her baby. Very soon, she will have that beautiful baby in her arms.

Once her pregnancy moved along, she returned home to be with her husband and prepare for the baby. By the time you read this, Kanti will have a baby. It is illegal to know the gender of the baby before birth, so we do not know what she will have. You will have to send me an email if you want to know the truth :)

Kanti has blessed us. It has nothing to do with us and more to do with just simple opportunity. Kanti came to us fragile, broken, lonely, and destitute. But today she is a strong wife, mother, friend. She is a strong woman. Not because of anything we have done. But because of the great God that allowed us to be there for her and provide her with a small opportunity. Kanti did the rest.

Update: Kanti had a baby boy.

Chapter 33

Jesus Toffee

Right before Christmas, we had a couple of friends stop in to see us. They were touring around and wanted to stop in. We had a good visit from Larry and Mark. They had been here a couple of years before, but they were unsure if any of the boys remembered them or not.

 I asked one of the boys if they recognized our friends and he said, "Oh yes Papa, these are the Jesus Toffee men." Jesus Toffee men? What in the world are you talking about??

We had no clue what they meant. When I asked him, he said that when the men were here before they handed out Jesus toffee. We still had no clue what he was talking about. He said that the men had given out candy hooks that were red and white. The red was for the blood of Jesus, and the white was for forgiveness.

At that moment we all belly laughed when we realized the boy was talking about candy canes. The trip before Larry and Mark had given the boys candy canes and told them what the stripes meant. Our boys never forget anything. Years later they still remember the story that Mark and Larry had told them, and they had not forgotten about the Jesus Toffee!

Chapter 34

Grandma Judy

I have mentioned Kiokee Baptist Church many times now, more than any other church. This is because their church members have visited us six times so far. We feel an intense bond with them primarily because of their presence. They don't just pray for us. Their prayers put on work clothes and join us in our "fields of harvest." One of my prayers is that we have the same relationships with other churches, too, because our boys need all the loving they can get.

I want to take the time to highlight one specific story about a Kiokee member that changed my life. You may remember from my book "Bear Believe Hope Endure" that I was introduced to Kiokee Baptist Church from my high school friend Michelle West Parnell. She had me speak at her WMU class, where I met some awesome ladies. One of those was Marcia Bailey, who led the first Kiokee trip to our children's home. After her trip, she invited me to come to speak to her Senior Citizen Sunday School Class. These are my favorite people. I don't feel worthy or equipped to stand and speak to a group of people with so much wisdom and life experience.

But I love it. The morning I spoke to Marcia's class, I spoke in general about our boys and how God is providing for us and how He will use them one day. When I was finished, I went to walk away, but God gave me a lightning bolt thought that I had to share. I told the class that we didn't need any more young adults to come over because we had always had plenty of that. I told them that our need wasn't for middle-aged people to come over and be aunts and uncles to our boys. All of that is wanted. But I shared with them that our greatest need is for our children to have grandparents. That is the one demographic that is missing on the teams to India. I told them about how special it was that Marcia and her sister had come over and been "Mimi" for our boys. I challenged them that if they were physically able, they should come over and love our boys. "Please do not rob our boys of their chance to hear your life experiences." I sat back down. What I didn't realize was that God had been working at that exact moment. In the room was a sweet woman named Judy Watkins. Judy was 84 years old. She sat there and thought about the need for grandmothers for our boys. She also remembered that God had called her to missions when she was 16 years old, but she never followed through. Life happened, and she got married and had kids and got into the swing of life. She had forgotten that promise and calling from when she was 16. But God had not forgotten. He was still calling her. Something inside of Mrs. Judy was telling her that she had to come to India on the next trip. She later told me that on her way home from church that day, she was so consumed with what to do that she got lost in thought. Before long, she was driving somewhere that she didn't expect. She was thinking so hard that she didn't drive home and was lost. She called her 60-year-old daughter and told her she was lost. Not sure of what might have caused it, her daughter asked if she was ok and if she needed her to come to get Mrs. Judy. Mrs. Judy responded that she was in her right mind but was consumed with the thought of this trip. She felt led to go, but how could she at 84 years old. Her daughter encouraged her to follow through and answer the call to missions that God had placed in her almost 70 years before. So Mrs. Judy said yes! It is important to mention here that Mrs. Judy's husband was 92 and in very poor shape. When the trip arrived, she had just shifted him to a nursing home. He began to go downhill, but she was still committed to fulfilling her promise to God. She told her daughter that if her husband Chester, did pass away not to tell her until she returned from India. It was only an 8-day trip anyway, and there would be nothing she could do. So Mrs. Judy came to India. She loved our boys as no one else had. And she was christened with a new name. She was now Grandma Judy. She was vibrant and full of l

Chapter 35

Thoughts from "Ken Uncle"

This chapter was submitted By Kenneth O'Barr, a current NLO Board member and dear friend. He has visited us three times so far with many more trips in the future.

April 2017

When I first heard about the team from Kiokee going to India, my first thought was "well, I've been to many other crazy places in the world, so why not go to India?". A lot of folks would say "I'm not going to India...it's not safe...it's So dirty....they hate Christians...the foods too spicy....I don't speak the language...the flight is so long...it's Too hot "....and so forth. In the end, those are just excuses. They aren't actual reasons you shouldn't go to India to be an encouragement to an amazing family of boys.

The preparation for the trip was somewhat tiresome. It does require significant time and effort to plan a trip across the globe with a group. However, once we arrived, it was one of the best experiences of my life. The boys were not in school, so we were able to spend at least 2 hours each day doing VBS activities and recreation. The boys also spent many hours each day harvesting wheat, so I spent a lot of time with the younger boys who were not able to work in the fields. One of our group members is a master woodworker, so he was able to work with a few of the older boys and teach them how to make tables or benches. A few of the ladies helped the boys learn to do some basic sewing such as sewing on a button. Viktar learned to crochet and quickly began making a blanket.

We did have an opportunity to visit the Taj Mahal on the way back to the airport. It was definitely good to see one of the oldest man-made wonders of the world. Other sightseeing during the week included Jaipur and Kesroli Fort. I skipped the trip to Jaipur because the main purpose of the trip was to ride elephants and I had already done that in Thailand. Kesroli Fort was a beautiful place to see, and it was fun to see a local community. I didn't really enjoy sleeping there, but the food was good. It is very close to Shiloh, so it is an easy excursion. Definitely take some time to see it in the daylight if you have the chance.

I really wasn't positive about my particular role on this trip. We had our pastor, our builder, our seamstress, our VBS leader, etc. What was my job? I can't play an instrument, I don't have any particular talents, so what exactly could I contribute? After returning home, processing my thoughts about the trip, and listening to Andy share his thoughts, I was able to understand that my role was to simply spend time with the boys, have fun with them, and encourage them. Andy told me that was most important to him. He said the boys need to feel loved. He also said, having teams come visit "makes the world a smaller place for the boys." So if you aren't sure how you could help a team on a trip to India, keep that in mind. Anyone can sit down with a kid and play a game, throw a frisbee, color a picture, or simply give the boys an encouraging smile. When we left at the end of the week, I was definitely heartbroken. I really enjoyed my time with the staff and the boys, and I did not want to leave. I knew I had to come back again.

In the meantime....

Between April and December, I had the opportunity to go with Andy to various festivals and sell items for Chunky Junk, White Peacock, and LOVOSO. This was a great experience for me because it helped me see firsthand what it takes to make the money needed to take care of the needs at Shiloh. During the festivals, we met so many different people from various walks of life. We were able to share about the work and ministry at Shiloh Children's Home. I invited Andy to come to the school where I teach. He was able to come in September and November to sell products from the three businesses. The teachers and staff were extremely supportive, and they helped the ministry of Shiloh through their purchases and donations. This did not take much effort from Andy or me. Anyone could invite Andy to set up a show at your home, school, or business. This type of sale doesn't really cost Andy anything but time, and the benefits for Shiloh are outstanding. The more people we can share with about the ministry, the more support will be created for it. Andy and Susan have a strong desire to be self-sustaining in their ministry. Through farming and selling handmade jewelry and pens, they are working toward that goal.

December Trip — Christmas and New Year's 2017–2018

In late May, about a month after I returned home from my first trip to visit Shiloh, I began

thinking about how I could go back to visit again and when that could happen. I was eating lunch with Andy and Susan and several other folks from Kiokee. I asked Andy when a good time would be to visit again. He said anytime during the summer or Christmas break since the boys would be out of school. So, I started asking other people about going to India for Christmas and New Year's. Most people said they couldn't miss Christmas with their families, so I figured I would just go alone. However, a few more people graciously agreed to go, and we booked our flights to New Delhi. As we worked through the planning process, I had several friends who asked me why I was going during the holidays. The simple answer was that I had time off from work, and I thought it would be fun to spend Christmas and New Year's with some really amazing people in India. Some folks just didn't understand how I could spend the holidays away from my family. So, I had to be a little more specific in my explanation. It's not the first time I have spent the holidays away from my family, so it didn't seem strange to me at all. I'm not married, and I don't have kids, so it is a little easier for me to be adventurous. My parents and my brother were very supportive of my decision. They are accustomed to my travel addiction. Plus, for us, Christmas is not about sitting around a tree and getting excited about what we got for Christmas. Christmas is about giving — not getting. I saw this as an opportunity to give. It ended up being the best Christmas of my life, and I'd love to do it again. I have no doubt it was a memorable Christmas for the boys and the staff at Shiloh.

For New Year's Eve, Andy purchased a massive amount of fireworks for the boys to enjoy. There were sparklers, spinners, firecrackers, and of course the large, soaring, booming fireworks. I think this was the only big fireworks display in the community. It lasted about 30 minutes and created a spectacular show for everyone. It was so much fun watching the boys dance around the spinners and trying to avoid them at the same time. The entertaining fireworks display ended with the lighting of 10,000 firecrackers. Yes, TEN THOUSAND! The strand looked to be at least 25 feet long. It was lit from both ends, and it steadily exploded, working its way toward the middle. It became increasingly louder, and everyone watching slowly moved backward a few steps to avoid the debris. By the time it ended, it sounded more like a war zone than a fireworks show. The boys loved every minute of it!

General thoughts....

If you ever have the chance to visit Shiloh Children's Home, you should jump at the opportunity. You won't regret it. It will be an unforgettable experience for you. Don't worry about the money, the "what if's," or anything else that may get in your way. God is bigger than all of those issues, and He will take care of everything. The staff and the boys will take great care of you, and they will love you deeply. It's what they do. In return, love them deeply. The boys love to laugh, play, sing, dance and enjoy life. Laugh and play with them. Sing and dance with them. Enjoy life with them.

You can't truly understand what daily life is like for them until you spend some time living with them. See the challenges they face. Hear the boys' 5:30 a.m. soothing acapella singing and the sound of everyone praying at the same time; or the sound of Surju's infectious laugh – you WILL laugh with him! Smell the various aromas all around you (there are plenty of those ☺). Taste the unique food and Susan's famous "white coffee." Feel love like you've never felt before. Hug and be hugged. Be a part of the most sincere worship and prayers you've ever experienced. Be a part of the family.

Chapter 36

Jaimie's Story

Even though Jaimie visited us in 2016, I thought her story would be a wonderful addition to this book. That experience taught me...

By: Jaimie D Sheth

I remember my first experience traveling to India. I was 16 years old, and it was the summer of 1992. I was excited and curious, but never nervous. I was going with my entire family, which included my parents and two brothers. We drove from Indiana, where we lived at the time, to Chicago to catch our flight to JFK, to Frankfort, to Bombay, and then finally to Ahmedabad, India where we would stay for one month. It was a debilitating journey; I had never been so tired.

My initial excitement stemmed from going to the country where my dad was born and where my mom and auntie grew up. In addition, I longed to meet my extended family; growing up in America, I was isolated from them, and now I wanted to hold close the idea of family after so many years without. My curiosity also stemmed from my interest in lesser developed countries, this one in particular, as it happened to be the seat of my heritage. Although my family and I had traveled quite a bit in the US and Canada, this would be my first major trip abroad. Similarities exist between the US and India, but differences are more apparent and significant.

Poverty is everywhere in the world, but homelessness in India is profound and very visible to anyone who goes there.

Pollution, at that time, was so intense, I would experience headaches every day I was there. The weather was so overwhelmingly hot, we spent most days in air-conditioned rooms trying to escape the heat, but we were fortunate, as most homes didn't have the luxury of cooling systems. However, as I was only 16, I didn't fully appreciate the magnitude of these issues until I had traveled to India for my fourth or fifth time.

It was this trip that showed me a lot about the poverty and levels of poverty that exists in India. When a little boy knocked on our car door seeking food or money, I thought my heart would break. His clothing was tattered, and he looked like he hadn't seen a proper shower or even water in weeks or months. My uncle got out of the car and went to the trunk where we had bags of leftover dinner from the restaurant we had just left. He gave it to this boy, who looked about five or six years old, as I watched him run to the median of the six-lane street we were driving on. There sat, what I presumed to be, his entire family of parents and siblings eating the leftover food my uncle had just given them. It was profound, sad, overwhelming, and educational all at the same time. That experience was an isolated real-life teaching about homelessness, specifically children who are without, poverty, prejudgment, and selfless giving, that I could never have learned in a book.

On my second visit to India four years later, I was 20 years old and had traveled to Ahmedabad again with my entire family. After leaving the first time, I remembered thinking I wasn't sure if I could handle another trip there. It's difficult not only physically, but emotionally, visually, and environmentally. After about three years, I completely forgot about all those aspects of traveling there, and I was eager and excited to go back. I wanted to see my extended family again and just be there with my parents and brothers. My dad booked the tickets for the following winter and off we went.

The visit was challenging like I had remembered; however, the pollution seemed a bit better, and the weather was nice as it was winter.

The poverty was as I remembered it, but my emotional response to it wasn't as profound. This fact enabled me to continue viewing it, but with the hope of helping to fix it.

I remember walking out of a women's dress shop with my dad one day when a little boy ran up to us and called my dad

"Kaka." In Gujarati, the language is predominantly spoken in Ahmedabad, Kaka means "Fathers brother," or in short, "Uncle," a respectful greeting children use for strangers. He wouldn't touch my dad, and he wasn't even bothersome or annoying. He was courteous and spoke to my dad like a friend.

He was a few steps ahead of us as we walked along a dirt road towards our car. He looked about the same age as the little boy I encountered in the middle of the street several years back, and he kept asking my dad for money. My dad reached into his pocket and gave him five Indian rupees, which at that time, was equivalent to about seven cents USD. That little boy took that money, looked at it as if it was gold, put both of his hands in his pockets, and had a spring in his step as he walked away from us. I remember constantly looking back at him, for I was so shocked about how happy he seemed. That experience taught me about the simplicities in life. It's not what or how much you give someone as long as you are giving, and the value of something can differ vastly from one individual to another. I met that little boy twenty-two years ago, and I will never forget him.

In 2016, I visited India for the eighth time. I had several reasons for my trip, including visiting family, meeting up with friends, and most of all, meeting Andy and Susan Lepper for the first time. I met Andy through a mutual friend years earlier, and he actually helped me form my nonprofit foundation in 2015 without really knowing me. I have a passion for kids, and after remember those two little boys I met on the streets in India, I was happy to know Andy and his wife Susan had this orphanage for boys.

It takes a special heart to do what Andy and Susan do for these boys. It was an adventure getting to the orphanage from Delhi with Andy and several of my friends. It was nice because I was able to get to know Andy, more so than the few messages we exchanged via Facebook messenger, and my friends were able to meet and get to know him for the first time along that journey to the home. Once there, I met Susan and the boys. Some were shy at first, and others came right up to us and were inquisitive. Different personalities to all of them, you felt the sense of brotherhood and family from 45 plus boys who are not blood-related.

We were only able to stay for a couple of days, but they were filled with seeing what life is like for these boys. I loved the chickens and the self-sustainable atmosphere the orphanage was trying to establish. I was happy not only to see how much love filled the home, but I felt it every day I was there through the actions of the entire team involved with caring for those boys. We were lucky to be witnesses to the unveiling of the new jungle gym that was donated. It was great seeing the boys so happy and realizing what they were just given. They have a good life. When seeing what it is like for the poor and homeless in India, especially the children, Andy and Susan provide a loving, caring, and stable home for these boys. I loved playing with them, listening to them, sitting with them to eat their favorite meal (noodles), and shopping for them. The interactions and experiences were beautifully overwhelming at times.

I was honored to be invited to the Shiloh home and to meet the No Longer Orphans family finally. That experience taught me about how, in many cases, less is more, about how the word "family" isn't defined by only one meaning, how there is strength in numbers, and finally, how one person (or in this case two), can change someone's life forever (or in this case 45-plus boys).

Section 6:
God's Provisions

Chapter 37

Good Things Come 12-20-13

There's a saying that says good things come to those who wait. We do a lot of waiting here at the orphanage. We have all but stopped sharing our daily needs, but we are relying on God to meet those needs. We spend a lot of time in prayer letting God know what we think our needs are. And then we wait.

That is some nervous excitement right there. Knowing that God will provide but wondering how exactly He will do it. I won't go into any details but suffice it to say that we have been running low on resources and have had to be really creative this last week on making ends meet.

Enter in God's creative intervention. On three consecutive days, people from our community came by to lend a helping hand and provide for the children. On the first day, two young and hip couples showed up with a bunch of treats for the children to celebrate Christmas. They passed out gulab jamun, samosas, and Parle G biscuits to the boys.

The next day, an officer in the army that was stationed close by came in to say that he was moving. He gave us two huge boxes of winter clothing for the boys. Finally, yesterday, an anonymous man came by and gave us enough money to buy chicken for the boys. As soon as he showed up, he was gone again. We didn't even catch his name. That makes it even better.

None of these gifts set the world on fire, but it provided exactly what we needed at that moment. It didn't leave us in abundance, but it was exactly what we needed. Just as God provided manna to the Israelites in their time of need, these gifts were our manna for that day.

Chapter 38

God Ain't Forgot Us Yet

If you haven't noticed already, we don't make it a habit of asking for money. We do have something called Project 450 that supports the boys, but fundraising is not our first focus. It is our belief that God is in control and He is the one providing for our every need. In turn, we give Him the glory for everything, not our brilliant social media or marketing campaigns.

This, of course, doesn't mean that we don't have needs. Boy, do we ever! Our response is to encourage people to ask God how they should be involved instead of us telling them how they should be involved. This takes a lot more faith, but it is also humbling seeing exactly how God provides.

A couple of days ago we had a need, so I specifically prayed for it. Susan called me later that night and said someone anonymously sent $25 in cash to our P.O. BOX in the United States. No name. No return address. That amount was almost to the penny of what I had prayed for. Thank you, Mr. or Mrs. Anonymous, and thanks be to God for hearing my ever-simple prayer.

Today is January 14. It is a holiday all over India sometimes known as Kite Day. It is one of the major festivals in the state of Rajasthan, known as "Makar Sankranti" or "Sankrant" in the Rajasthani language. This day is celebrated with some special Rajasthani delicacies and sweets like Pheeni (either with sweet milk or sugar syrup dipped),Til-paati, Gajak, kheer, Pakodis, Puwas, Til-ladoos, etc. "

God knew that our supplies were running low because five different groups of people have come by and dropped off food for the children. Five groups of people!!! Man, what a blessing! It started out this morning with a family bringing a full breakfast for the children. Then, someone brought a bunch of pantry items like flour, sugar, salt, and other spices. Another came by and brought A LOT of bananas.

No sooner had they left, a man on a motorcycle stopped and gave the children sweet treats, peanuts, and sesame seed treats. He gave them each a pencil case with school supplies, and as he was still passing out the treats, ANOTHER guy showed up to give the children salty snacks and sweet treats. It all happened this morning in a short amount of time. It would not surprise me if a few other people showed up between now and bedtime.

What a joy it is to know that not only is God providing for us, but we also get to spend some time with our community that truly has a heart for the well-being of these boys. God hasn't forgotten us. Our needs are great, even overwhelming most of the time, and our reliance on Him has never been greater. Seeing the way He provides gives me a greater peace than I could ever create for myself or the boys. We will keep praying and God will keep providing. Join us in this prayer.

Chapter 39

Sometimes it's the Little Things

Grace and mercy can be extended at times and from places you least expect. God is surely looking out for us. He surely hasn't forgotten us yet.

We have an awesome grocery shop here in the city called Easy Way. It is actually owned by the mighty Wal-Mart. It basically has the same things that you would find at a Dollar General or Family Dollar in the United States with the inclusion of produce and frozen items. I buy a lot of my personal supplies there. The staff is super friendly and know me by name.

A few months ago, I invited a couple of workers to come visit us. They obliged and also brought some rice for the boys. Yesterday, as I was leaving the shop, I noticed they had purged their produce for the day and it was in a couple of small shopping carts next the dumpster out front. I asked the manager what he did with the day-old produce and he said they either toss it or give it to the sacred cows. Even in India they are throwing away day-old produce!!!

I asked him if he would give it to our orphans because

I think they are sacred and we would really like all of the fresh vegetables. He asked me if I was sure. The truth is, the vegetables we can buy here in our small village outside of the city are actually worse looking than the ones he was about to throw away. I imagine that our vegetables here in our village are probably a week past their prime, not a day. I told him that it was a blessing for him to give the food to our boys and he agreed. I already bought so much before noticing this that I didn't have enough space on my motorcycle to carry it. I asked him when we could come by again and he told me to come at 11 a.m. the next day.

That was this morning. Around 11 a.m., I was knee-deep in problems here. Our power keeps surging and going out, and the pump for our well finally died. I was busy trying to get an electrician to come here and fix the problem. Needless to say, the time slipped by me and I didn't even notice.

At 12 p.m., I got a call on my cell. I thought it was the electrician. It wasn't. It was the produce man from Easy Way. He was calling to ask me if I was coming. I told him I would be there as soon as I possibly could. The cool thing was that I hadn't given him my number. To my knowledge, no one at the store has it. He called around to other shopkeepers until he found someone who knew me and acquired my number from him. He tracked me down and took the time to call and let me know he had saved the veggies for us.

When I got there, I was pleasantly surprised. I am not really sure exactly how much was there, but I would estimate that it was a good fifty pounds, divided into two large potato sacks that I had to bring back on my bike. Nicodemus went with me, so he had a twenty-five pound bag in his lap while I balanced the second bag on my gas tank and between my handlebars. I had to drive very slow and still had a few "close encounters of the Indian traffic kind."

The best part is that the manager came out and told me he is willing to give us the produce every day if we are willing to come get it. I am glad the regulations for this kind of thing are different than they are in the United States; otherwise, I doubt we could jump through the paperwork hoops to get it done. Even if this is a short-term kind of thing, I am blessed and happy to know we have new friends looking out for us and that our boys will get some great veggies at a pleasant price :)

Here is a list of what we received:
- cilantro
- tomatoes
- capsicum
- potatoes
- gourd
- mangoes
- pumpkins
- okra
- cucumbers
- lemons

Chapter 40

God Shows Up

Even in the midst of our hardships, God shows up. Today, in between visits by government officials, we put up some Christmas decorations. Now the boys are signing all of your Christmas cards. It's been a very rough week. A group of boys were standing under the decorations and belly laughing. They all said, "Papa, Christmas is coming!" None of these boys were with us last year, and it hit me hard that this is the first Christmas they have ever had. Makes a grown man get choked up thinking about it. After a week of fighting with people who would rather see us close up and these boys back on the streets, it's overwhelming when God shows up. This is why we do what we do.

Chapter 41

Never Going Hungry

This is one of those hard to believe stories. But trust me that it is entirely true. It feels like it is borrowed from the pages of George Meuller's autobiography, but I attest that it happened to us. In 2015 there were 54 times where at some point during the day we wouldn't have enough food to eat. You didn't misread that. There wasn't a typo. 54 times.

If you do the math, that is right at once per week. So, on an average of once per week for a whole year, we were put in a situation of going without food. But this is not from neglect or lack of planning. In fact, we try extra hard for this never to happen. That is why we grow wheat, corn, mustard, and other crops. It is why we have goats, chickens, ducks, geese, and water buffaloes. There were times where our city was on strike, and although we had money for food, there was no way to get it. There were times of monsoon where the markets were flooded. There were so many ways in which we had made plans to fill our pantry, but it was still barren. 54 times without enough food to survive.

But can you guess how many meals our children missed? The

answer is zero. Even though there were 54 times that we were without food, there was not a single time that we missed a meal. But how?

Let me start by saying that I believe these small acts of miracles were done for a particular time to recalibrate us towards a God-centered focus. I truly believe that God did it "this way" to bring Himself more glory. So, any preparation on our part was futile anyway. This was apparent when we would buy extra monthly rations, but they would still run out.

It was like the reverse of the story of Elijah and the widow in 1 Kings chapter 17. In that story, God replenished her flour and oil every night. She never ran out as God had promised. For us, it was the opposite. We would close and lock our store room confident that we had enough food for the following day, only to open again and realize the food would run out long before we filled all our hungry bellies. It felt like food would vanish in the night. But that was highly unlikely. We always locked the storeroom, and I was the only one who had the key. And every time we discovered that we were lacking, it was soon followed by small acts of kindness.

We have had times where people would show up without warning to provide breakfast for the children. We have had local shops call us to tell us they had a donation of food for us. We even have a local vegetable vendor who would randomly give us all the leftover vegetables at the end of the day. But we never knew when it was coming.

Don't forget our animals. We have chickens mainly for the eggs and the water buffaloes for their milk. There were so many days that the chickens just simply didn't give any eggs, or gave a minuscule amount, only to be inundated the following day with more eggs than we needed. The same was true for the water buffalo and the milk. I can say that there were days where it just didn't make sense that there was no food available. But in every situation, God provided in miraculous ways, and our boys never went hungry. It became a challenge to figure out how God would provide for us and we welcomed it, knowing that God would meet our needs.

I want to share with you one story in particular. Bear in mind that not every child knew that we had these struggles with food. Some of our boys come from poor backgrounds, and the last thing I wanted was for the smaller boys to be food insecure, wondering where the next meal would come from. That is our responsibility, and we didn't want them to worry. But we have made some of the times aware to the older boys so they could pray accordingly. One morning I woke up to discover that our pantry was bare and we had nothing for breakfast other than spices. I called 5 of the older boys aside and told them the situation. I asked them if they would join me in prayer and they agreed.

We sat down and began to pray. I was just getting warmed up when they got up and started to leave. I asked them why they were leaving so soon, and one boy responded, "Don't worry Papa. God will provide. We know he will. We believe He will, so we are going to get ready for school." I wasn't as convinced quite yet, so I decided to pray as I walked around the building. The boys would soon be leaving for school, so I went to our front gate and unlocked the thick chain.

No sooner had I walked back to our front door did a small car come screaming through the front entrance. The way the car came to a stop, I was sure that the driver used to be a stuntman on The Dukes of Hazzard. He got out and quickly ran over to me. I was unsure of his intentions, so I positioned myself between him and our front door. He immediately said, "Sir, you have to help me." I was so confused but curious about what this man wanted at such an early hour. It was a little after 6am, and the sun had risen not long before. "Please help me sir or my wife will kill me." I asked him what in the world he meant. He told me that he had gone to the vegetable market bright and early to get his families fresh food for the day. He had also picked up a bag of rice. As he was driving home, he noticed that there were two bags of rice in the back. He told me that his wife would never believe that he didn't buy it and that someone accidentally put it back there when they were loading up the other bag. He told me that from experience he knew that his wife would fight with him and he just didn't want to deal with it. So he asked me if I would please take it. I told him that I would gladly take it because we were not sure where our daily food would come. He gladly handed it over, and he was on his way.

But before he got in the car, I had one question to ask. I said, "What made you stop here? I have not seen you before. Why did you come to us?" He told me that he had stopped along the side of the road and got out to put the rice on the side.

He knew that someone would come along and take it and he wouldn't have to explain anything to his wife. But then he said, "As I was about to take the rice out, I noticed the sun shining through the plus sign on the top of your building.

Something inside told me that the "plus sign people" would take my rice. So, I came to you, and you took it."

Once again God had provided in a miraculous way for us. He used a non-Christian passerby to provide our daily food. The man had noticed the cross on our building, and God used him to provide for us. And by the way, it wasn't just a small bag of rice. It was a 50-kilogram bag of rice which is 110 pounds. SO not only did he provide our daily meal, but we ate for days off of that one act of kindness.

Through 2015 we had crazy ups and downs. But God showed up in miraculous ways, each time letting us know that we were loved and that he was taking care of us. We have not had any days without food in many months, but God has cemented in our hearts and minds how far He will go to meet our daily needs.

Chapter 42

New Well

I was in the United States traveling in Mid-December when Susan called me. She said we had a problem with our well. This was not good. We have had issues with vandalism of our well in the past. Our well was dug over a decade ago, and for some unknown reason, they decided to dig it in the middle of one of our fields. It was not strategic. First, it was not strategic because it was in the middle of the field. The tractor always had to be careful around it.

But most importantly, it wasn't the right place because it was so far away from our building that people could vandalize it without us being aware. The old well was 300 feet deep. At the very bottom of the shaft was an electric pump that would send water from the well through a pipeline to a storage tan closer to our building. Once our storage tank was full, we would turn on a motor there that would fill individual tanks on our roof that were connected to our bathrooms and kitchens. So we never had water on demand. Our building has six tanks on the roof that each hold about 500 gallons of water. So you only have access to the amount of water that is in any given tank. When your water runs out of that tank, it can be refilled by turning on the motor from our storage tank. The biggest problem with vandalism was the way that the well was set up. With the motor being at the bottom of the 300-foot shaft, it meant that we had to run 300 feet of electrical wire from the ground down to the bottom to pump water out. Somewhere angry neighbors realized that the best way to upset us was to cut that electrical line from the top. At least half a dozen times people cut the wire and let the remaining line fall to the bottom of the well. This means that to power the pump at the bottom, we had to remove ALL 300 feet of pipe to bring up the pump at the bottom. We would rewire it and install it at the bottom of the 300 foot well. This came at the cost of $500 each time because we had to rent a crane big enough to remove all of the pipes. It was a design flaw and we just never got around to building a locked structure around it.

So, when Susan told me that we had a problem with our well, the first thing I thought of was that someone had cut the line again. But I was shocked when she said that the problem wasn't vandalism; the problem was the well had run completely dry. I knew that we had a bad year as far as the rains and the monsoon. We didn't have near enough rain as years past. But December is the cool time. I didn't think it would run dry. This was a significant problem because we had just planted our wheat and mustard in the fields. Not to mention that 50 people and 500 animals rely on that water to survive each day. We needed water, and we needed it fast! I mentioned the need on social media. Within 6 hours we had gifts of $15,000 to cover the cost of a new well. Many people gave, and we are thankful to all. But we are especially grateful to Westview Baptist Church in West Virginia that gave selflessly and abundantly so that the kids could have clean drinking water. At first, we thought we would only need $6,000, but boy were we wrong. We didn't doubt God when He provided us with $15,000, but we didn't know why. We knew that it would take a few days to get the well dug because the well diggers were busy. So we immediately rented tanker trucks full of water for our fields and the building. Because of the previous vandalism, we decided to dig the new well a lot closer to the building. What we thought would take two days ended up taking 10. The well diggers had to progressively rent bigger and bigger machines because nothing seemed to work. We had wanted to dig a 500 foot well, but we had to settle for 285 feet. At one point we had made it to 200 feet deep when we hit a virtually unbreakable rock. The crew worked feverishly to try to break it but got increasingly frustrated. They were ready to quit for good, but we begged them to wait so we could have time to pray. All of the boys and staff gathered and prayed and soon after the rock broke in pieces. We were so thankful that we made it to 285 feet. We begged the workers to try longer but they just wouldn't. We called in experts to access the situation. They confirmed to us that this well should provide us with clean water for the foreseeable future. So, for now, we have fresh water. We also built a pump house complete with a door and lock to keep the vandals away. The final cost was precisely $15,000 once all was said and done. God knows what He is doing and the sooner we trust that the better and more at peace we will be.

Section 7:
From Our Hearts

Chapter 43

Confession Time

I have a confession to make. I have a favorite donation. How dare I say that in this politically correct world! You can't show favorites! Everyone should get a trophy, right? Well, this isn't exactly like a participation trophy. Let me explain. I will not name names;).

We have had donations of up to $5000 from single donors, and everywhere in between, but my favorite donation is $8. I will not say who it's from, but they have been giving to the boys long-term. I have no clue why it's $8. Seems like such a random amount. Maybe that's why it's so intriguing. I have come up with many theories through the years as to why $8.

Why not $5 or $10? Why $8? Is it because the donor had exactly that to give the first time they gave and has kept it that way? Is it because that is an equal portion of the tithes and offerings per month? Is the number symbolic? I may never know. Truthfully, I don't want to know. To me it symbolizes three things and that's why it's so memorable:

1. It's a weird amount. It's not standard and that's ok. Because I am weird and so are our boys. You may not realize it, but you are weird too and that's ok. Even the Bible calls us "peculiar people". Weird sticks out. It's memorable and that's what we strive to be for the boys and pray that that is what they become also.

2. It's a small amount. It is our smallest donation. It pales in comparison to some gifts and represents the boys perfectly. They are small and deemed as insignificant. It's like the tortoise and the hare. The unexpected sneaks up on you and ends up surprising you. Our boys are going to surprise this world and do great things. And we like it that way.

3. Small things can make a big difference. Over the course of our ministry, this $8 monthly gift keeps coming, month after month. And it keeps adding up. The full amount over the course of more than two years represents many things. It represents the purchase of at least two goats. Or 200 chickens. Or a used motorcycle. Or almost a year of food for one of our boys. Continuity matters. If you don't quit, your life will have more purpose. This is what we teach the boys. Like the widow's mite, success, worship, and giving is not judged by the amount as much as the heart. The world may view our boys as not having much to give, but we know the Bible teaches us that small things given with the heart have lasting impact. Thank you, $8 donor, for teaching us such beautiful lessons.

Chapter 44

One of the Greatest Days of My Life

You remember certain days more than others. Some you want to remember, and some you want to forget. I want to forget the many days I learned that someone close to me had passed. In that very moment and day, I wasn't concerned with their eternal security. I was mourning the hole they left in my heart. I was hurting for what was taken from me. I am selfish, and loss hurts. You learn to deal with it, but my initial reaction is always sadness and confusion. I still haven't come to grips with death.

Someone once told me to just "get over it. Death is natural and all a part of life." Well, it doesn't feel natural to me for a thirty-five-year-old father and husband to be taken so early. I don't doubt God for a moment, but I just don't understand it. And it feels horrible.

Luckily, those days are few and the good far outweighs the bad. The days I want to remember are the ones of joy. I want to remember my special birthdays, and I do. I also remember my wedding day like it happened hours ago. I remember certain days here with our Shiloh boys that I will cherish forever.

One day in particular has become the greatest day of my life. It was September 18, 2015. That was the day my wife gave birth to our first son. Four times every second, all around the world, a baby is born. The circumstances surrounding the birth of my son make it the greatest thing to ever happen to me. My feelings are intensified because of the buildup to the birth. That is an epic story all unto itself.

You see, my wife and are not newly married. I am not old, but I sure ain't no spring chicken. I am pushing forty and my wife and I have been married for thirteen years. Not exactly the time to have your first child, but that wasn't by design.

We were married in India in 2003 in front of 1,500 orphans. We tried from the beginning to start our family. We tried. And we tried. And. We. Tried. But nothing. Days turned into weeks, weeks into months, months into years. I wasn't exactly young when we were first married, so I thought I was ready. In India, you have kids as soon as you are married. A young couple on our staff had a baby ten months after their wedding day. That is all too common. But we waited.

We felt the pressure from our Indian friends and family. They made us feel as if it were a choice for us to wait. There was no choice whatsoever. I have been dreaming of being a father since I was young. I wanted to be the type of father that my father was to me. I wanted to carry on the legacy. I also felt outside pressure even though it was unintentional. I am the only male on my father's side of the family. I have a sister and four female cousins. I felt the burden of carrying on the Lepper name. Laugh all you want at the name, but men of endless integrity and deep convictions have carried this name.

It is an honor to be a Lepper. I wear the name like a badge of honor, so naturally I felt the burden of passing it on.

It seemed it wasn't meant to be. We went to fertility specialists in the United States and in India. Some couldn't see any problem, but most said there was no chance of getting pregnant. We both were tested and found out that the problem wasn't mine. That broke my heart. I can take the pain of it being my fault, but I just couldn't take it that Susan felt it was her fault. What a helpless feeling! Susan continued to go to various doctors, all having conflicting and somewhat confusing advice. We held out hope that God would heal her and knew that it would take a miracle.

I began to shut down and suppress the desire to have my own child. This was about the time we took over leadership of the Shiloh Children's Home. Meeting these boys for the first time filled a void in my heart that I tried to suppress. Very quickly, these kids became more than boys; they became my sons. That was enough, (and still is).

Maybe it was the receding of our stress level, or maybe it was because the Shiloh boys made us a Papa and Mommy for the first time, but either way, we fell in love and we had indescribable peace. But God wasn't finished. He heard our prayer and He was about to answer. Secretly, Susan was still holding out hope. It wasn't like she was hiding, but she had continued to secretly take pregnancy tests holding out hope.

On the morning of February 10, at 4 a.m., Susan woke me up by tapping me on the cheek. She kept saying, "I peed! I peed." I congratulated her and asked if I could go back to sleep.

"Wake up you idiot! I think I am pregnant!" Through crusty eye boogers, I noticed the pee stick with which she had been tapping me on the cheek. It showed two straight pink lines. I couldn't believe it.

I wanted to believe it, but my hope had been wavering for so long. I called my best friend Jason who is a trauma surgeon. He told us that there were no false positives with pregnancy tests, so it was likely true, but encouraged us to go to a doctor for confirmation. Later that day, Susan did just that and it was confirmed. We were going to be parents.

I will save the full story for another book, but on September 18, 2015, we welcomed Andrew Michael Lepper Jr. into the world. We decided to call him Micah. It had been decades since we had separately prayed for a child and thirteen years since we started praying together. I still can't believe we have a son!

I want to candidly share this with you — my love for Micah is no greater and no less than it is for our other forty-five boys. It is just different because of how God answered the prayer of our hearts after praying for so long. Likewise, my love for these forty-five boys is different because of how God called us here and made the way possible. I can sit and hold Micah and cry because of how faithful God is. At the same time, I can sit and hold Mohit and cry because of the circumstances of why he is here. I love Mohit more than words can express. My heart breaks when I think of the mother that abandoned him on our doorsteps. To be able to hold him and to be the only father Mohit knows is a responsibility I don't take likely.

I actually had a couple of people ask me if we would move back to the United States now that Micah was born. They went on to say now that we had our own child, surely the void was filled in our hearts. Excuse me? We have not sacrificed everything we have ever known to come reduce these orphans to fill a void in our hearts! And we surely wouldn't turn right around and abandon them all over again because we had our own child.

Seriously? I just do not understand, and I guess I never will. I have even had adoptive parents tell me that I should have separation between the rest of the orphans and me, Micah, and Susan. Oh really? Is that what people do also with children they have adopted? On one hand, we have left everything we have ever known in the United States. We left our jobs, our homes, our family, and our friends. Not to mention Chick Fil A. We didn't do this to become guardians or dorm parents. We are not an uncle and auntie to the boys. When we left everything, we did it because these boys needed a father and mother.

Might I add here that I actually do not feel or believe that we have made a sacrifice of any kind. People may count what we have given up to serve these boys, but to us it is not a loss. When David Lingstone was asked about the sacrifice of leaving England to serve in Africa his response was this, "It is emphatically no sacrifice. Say rather it is a privilege. Anxiety, sickness, suffering, or danger, now and then, with a foregoing of the common conveniences and charities of this life, may make us pause, and cause the spirit to waver, and the soul to sink; but let this only be for a moment. All these are nothing when compared with the glory which shall be revealed in and for us. I never made a sacrifice." And so it is with Andy and Susan Lepper. When it comes to rescuing and serving these orphans, we have never made a single sacrifice. NOT.EVEN. ONE.

These kids have been abandoned by every single person they have ever known. I empathize with their families that have left them here because they felt they had nothing to offer. We do have something to offer. And we do have a void in our hearts. But it's a God-shaped hole. That cannot be filled in with any relationship in the world. Wealth can't fill it. Neither came fame or status. This God-shaped hole can be filled by laying our life down to bring glory to God. This is different for everyone. God has called us here not as travelers or missionaries, or buddies for these boys.

We are here as Papa and Mommy. No offense intended, but you can have your mission trips. We don't want them. We don't want a trip dedicated to missions. We want a life dedicated to missions. We love, care for, and provide for these boys with every fiber of our being. Some may come and go at no fault of our own. They may grow up and leave or have a family member come and take them back. That doesn't stop them from always being my boys. Your love must not be a reflection of someone's reaction to your love. Your love must be unconditional. It has no strings attached. And love has no motives. I am here because of my deep love for God and these boys, not because I have ulterior motives or any expectations for them.

My sincerest prayer is that they become true worshippers, but I will love them regardless of their reaction to my love. Haven't you had relationships where the love was uneven? Maybe you loved someone with a different intensity than they loved you. Maybe you loved them long before that love was reciprocated. I feel that daily. The levels of love shown me from the boys can be as different as extreme hugs and affection from one boy to rejection and apathy from another. I don't love the apathetic child any less than the affectionate one.

In fact, it strikes the fire within even hotter to be the love that this boy may have never seen. If you have kids, maybe you can relate to the point that your love for each is equal but not the same. You may love the creativity of one child but the deep thinking of another. It's no greater or less love, it's just displayed differently. Maybe I am utterly naive and no one else will ever get it, but my love for Micah is not greater than my love for these orphans; It is just different.

One of the many reasons I love Micah is because he is the physical embodiment of God's faithfulness. Long ago, I stopped fervently praying for a child and was resigned to the fact that if it was to be then it would happen. I felt that I had prayed enough and that God would either give or He wouldn't. But Susan never stopped praying. God heard her prayer. The funny thing is, as I was too broken to even utter a prayer, Susan was proclaiming bold prayers. Everyone she told laughed at her and mocked her when she said she was praying for a blonde hair, blue eyed baby. Many believed that would never happen because of how dominant her India-ness is. I write to you today about God's answered prayer, not just for a baby, but one that on this very day still has blue eyes and little tufts of blonde hair. It seems too good to be true, but God did it.

We have begun joking with baby Micah that the reason it took

13 years for us to have him is because it took that long for God to find a blonde hair blue eyed Indian boy with such a sweet heart. He is quite the package. I am unabashedly his biggest fan, but this has to be one of the calmest babies ever. He RARELY ever cries. He is so content and calm.

And that is just what we needed. God knew that. I was reminded this week of the story of Lazarus. God has used it in a special way to speak to me. In case you are not aware of the story, I will keep it simple. Lazarus and Jesus were friends. In fact, people referred to Lazarus as the "one that Jesus loved." Lazarus became very sick and his sisters sent for Jesus. Jesus purposefully waited longer even though He probably wanted to be with His friend. Jesus exact words as found in John 11:4 are, "This sickness will not end in death, but is for the glory of God, so that the Son of God may be glorified through it."

After hearing that Lazarus was sick, Jesus waited two more days before he even started His journey. It's not like He was walking down the block. It took Him days to get to Lazarus. In fact, by the time He got there, Lazarus was not only dead, but had been buried for four days.

This didn't exactly sit well with Lazarus's sisters even though they loved Jesus. They asked him why he didn't come sooner. Mary said, "If you had been here sooner, my brother would not have died." Everyone was distraught and even Jesus wept. But as the Bible tells us, Jesus stood at the base of the tomb and called Lazarus out. He came to life and walked out of the tomb four days after being put inside the tomb dead. We can glean from this story that Jesus had the power to heal sickness, but instead He choose to heal death.

So, my question to you is, Was Jesus late, or was He right on time? Look back to what Jesus said when He found out that Lazarus was sick. He knew that the sickness would lead to death. But He also knew that He would raise Lazarus from that death.

The purpose??? "For the Glory of God." If this is the case, then God was not late. Jesus was not late. There was a purpose from the beginning of time for Lazarus. It was meant for his death and life to bring glory to God.

As I read this story, it strangely gave me comfort and peace that I had been missing for MANY years. Even after the birth of Micah, I still questioned God and His timing. Why had HE waited so long? What was the purpose? Quite simply, I can stand before you today and proclaim that God's timing is perfect. He is never late. Why did we have to endure hardship, longing, grief, and pain for thirteen years waiting on the birth of a child?

Because of the Glory of God. Plain and simple. No further explanation is needed. No translation will suffice. God was on time even when we didn't comprehend, and Micah's birt' and life points to God's Glory. Praise God, great things HE ' done. For this main reason, I celebrate the birth of my so' just because he is an answer to many prayers, but bec? birth brought glory to God!

Andrew M. Lepper

Chapter 45

The Weight of Struggles

It's not the weight of your struggle but how you carry it. This thought hit me like a brick in the face this past week. I was heading into town on my motorcycle as I do almost daily. It is a split road with a fence and some flowers in between the four lanes of traffic. My two lanes into town are not very wide. Passing isn't the easiest task on the best of days but it doable.

This was about 6 am. Otherwise, there would be bikes, cows, pigs, people, and cars galore.

And then I came upon him. An old man on a motorcycle that was visible struggling. He was carrying over 20 bamboo poles on his motorcycle each at least 10 feet long. First, let me say that I know how this guy may feel because I have firsthand knowledge. Not too long ago we were building a chicken coop, and I bought 30 of the same poles.

But the main difference is that I had someone to help me. Someone sat behind me on the bike and balanced the massive poles on their legs as the poles pointed straight ahead and behind. I cannot imagine ever thinking that balancing them on the back would be an option. At the very least you need someone there to help.

And that, my friends, is the point. If you are carrying the weight of your struggles by yourself, there is nothing bracing you from a fall. Someone to share the weight and balance it as you steer is crucial.

The Bible also speaks to this. 1 Peter 5:7 says, "Give all your worries and cares to God, for he cares about you." What is the point of doing it all yourself if you crash and burn? God cares for us. Give him what you are struggling to carry.

There is a saying that goes something like, "God will never give you more than you can handle." That sounds all warm and fuzzy, but I greatly disagree with it. If we could always handle what comes our way, we would never have a need for a Saviour, and we would never glorify Him when He rescues us. The truth is all He does is give us more than we can handle This way when the weight of our struggles become too much, we will turn to Him.

The truth is, if I can be transparent and vulnerable with you, I am feeling the weight of my struggles right now more than ever before. I am overwhelmed here at the children's home. We have very little support, and my family's personal savings are long gone. I am on fumes, and I can't do it anymore. I am ready to throw in the towel and admit defeat.

But this is precisely the time that I need to crawl into my savior's lap and trust that He has this. I am so exhausted I just need rest. In a sense, the poles on the back of my bike are

We Are Shiloh: Stories of the Shiloh Children's Home

about to make me crash and burn. But I know that I will never find rest in myself. No amount of free time or sleep can give me genuine rest. That only comes from God.

What struggles are you dealing with? How intense is that weight? The sooner you realize that God has your back and He is the only one who can handle this, the sooner you can give Him glory for who He is.

And finally, I waited around to see how the old man on the motorcycle would do. No more than 1 minute after the photo was snapped, 2 "random" men rode up in between us. Just from body language, I surmised that they probably didn't know each other. The guy on the back of the bike got onto the back of the old man's bike as the new driver placed the poles strategically on his leg. And then they were off. I am convinced that the old man didn't know the guy that helped him. But there he was sharing the burden and carrying the full brunt of the weight of the struggle.

God is approaching you and me also. Will we cast our burdens on Him and let Him carry our struggles? True rest is found there.

Chapter 46

Closing

Thank you for taking the time to weave through time and history with us. Thank you sharing our joy and laughter as you have read these stories. If any of these stories have resonated with you I invite you to join us at our website and on social media. We keep friends like you as up to date as we can. If you want to join our newsletter then send us an email and we will add you. Thank you for helping us to care for these precious souls. We could not do the ministry of No Longer Orphans without you.

Email: info@nolongerorphans.org

Website: www.nolongerorphans.org

Facebook: https://www.facebook.com/nlorphans

Instagram: @nolongerorphans

We Are Shiloh: Stories of the Shiloh Children's Home

Made in the USA
Columbia, SC
24 September 2020